Rasputin the Rascal Monk

Rasputin the Rascal Monk

William Le Queux

MINT EDITIONS

Rasputin the Rascal Monk was first published in 1917.

This edition published by Mint Editions 2021.

ISBN 9781513277806 | E-ISBN 9781513278216

Published by Mint Editions®

 MINT
EDITIONS
minteditionbooks.com

Publishing Director: Jennifer Newens
Design & Production: Rachel Lopez Metzger
Project Manager: Micaela Clark
Typesetting: Westchester Publishing Services

Contents

I

The Cult of the "Sister-Disciples"

The war has revealed many strange personalities in Europe, but surely none so sinister or so remarkable as that of the mock-monk Gregory Novikh—the middle-aged, uncleanly charlatan, now happily dead, whom Russia knew as Rasputin.

As one whose duty it was before the war to travel extensively backwards and forwards across the face of Europe, in order to make explorations into the underworld of the politics of those who might be our friends—or enemies as Fate might decide—I heard much of the drunken, dissolute scoundrel from Siberia who, beneath the cloak of religion and asceticism, was attracting a host of silly, neurotic women because he had invented a variation of the many new religions known through all the ages from the days of Rameses the Great.

On one occasion, three years before the world-crisis, I found myself at the obscure little fishing-village called Alexandrovsk, on the Arctic shore, a grey rock-bound place into which the black chill waves sweep with great violence and where, for four months in the year, it is perpetual night. To-day, Alexandrovsk is a port connected with Petrograd by railway, bad though it be, which passes over the great marshy tundra, and in consequence has been of greatest importance to Russia since the war.

While inspecting the quays which had then just been commenced, my friend Volkhovski, the Russian engineer, introduced me to an unkempt disreputable-looking "pope" with remarkable steel-grey eyes, whose appearance was distinctly uncleanly, and whom I dismissed with a few polite words.

"That is Grichka (pronounced Greesh-ka), the miracle-worker!" my friend explained after he had ambled away. "He is one of the very few who has access to the Tsar at any hour."

"Why?" I asked, instantly interested in the mysterious person whose very name the Russian Censor would never allow to be even mentioned in the newspapers.

My friend shrugged his broad shoulders and grinned. "Many strange stories are told of him in Moscow and in Petrograd," he said. "No doubt you have heard of his curious new religion, of his dozen wives of noble birth who live together far away in Pokrovsky!"

I glanced back at the receding shock-haired figure in the long black clerical coat and high boots, little dreaming that I had met the mock-Saint whose evil influence was to cause the downfall of the Imperial House of Romanoff.

Strange it is that to-day I have before me the amazing official reports of his career from revolutionary and private sources—reports from which I intend to here set out certain astounding facts.

First, it is quite beyond question that the Pravoslavny Church, with its malign influences and filthy practices, is, in the main, responsible for Gregory Novikh's success as a worker of bogus "miracles." The evil-minded libertine upon whom his fellow-villagers in Pokrovsky, in the Siberian Province of Tobolsk, bestowed the name of Rasputin (or in Russian, "Ne'er-do-well-son)," was a fisherman who possessed an inordinate fondness for the village lasses, and also for vodka. A mere illiterate mujik, disgusting in his habits and bestial in his manners, he grew lazy and dissolute, taking to theft and highway-robbery, for which, according to the official report of the Court of Tobolsk, before me, he was imprisoned twice, and a third time was publicly flogged and so degraded that he was compelled to bid farewell to Pokrovsky, much to the relief of the villagers. Behind him he left a peasant wife, a little son, named Dmitri, and two daughters. He also left behind him a handsome young peasant woman known as Guseva, a person who was destined to contribute a few years later in no small measure to his dramatic death. Sins always follow the sinners.

After a year or two of wandering as a rogue and vagabond, committing thefts where he could, and betraying any woman he came across, he suddenly conceived the brilliant idea of posing as a "holy man." This idea came to him because, while in Pokrovsky, he had had as boon companion and fellow-drunkard a certain market-gardener who had joined the Pravoslavny Church and is to-day by his influence actually a bishop!

In most Eastern countries, especially in India and China, there are many wandering "holy men," and modern Russia is no exception. To lead a "gospel life" of endless pilgrimages to "holy" places and to collect money for nonexistent charities appealed to the fellow as an easy mode of lazy sensual self-indulgence. Therefore he adopted it, being aided by the ex-market-gardener, who was already in the Church. So both prospered exceedingly well.

Rasputin had by this time discovered himself possessed of quite extraordinary powers. Indeed a report upon him written by a great Russian alienist who knew him intimately, has recently reached London, and from its voluminous pages which I have had before me, I gather that both physiologically and psychically he was abnormal, while his natural hypnotic influence was marked by the rare power he possessed of being able to contract the pupils of his steel-grey eyes at will, regardless of sunlight or shadow. Few persons can do this. It is a sign well known to alienists that the person is a criminal degenerate. Rasputin never smiled, even when he drank heavily. He could consume three bottles of champagne and still be quite sober! With vodka, his favourite spirit, he became talkative, but never indiscreet. He was a lunatic of an intensely erotic type; a satyr who possessed a truly appalling influence over women of all ages, and even at his word men in high positions did not hesitate to cast off their brilliant uniforms and decorations and mortify their flesh!

From this man, crafty, cunning and elusive, a fiendish satyr whose hypnotic influence was irresistible, no woman, however high-born, high-minded, or highly religious was safe. He lived upon his wits, and lived well. With that amazing cunning usual in such criminals he affected a deep piety, so that at the various monasteries where he sought hospitality he was welcomed. In Russia many of the religious houses still unfortunately savour of the most disgraceful debauchery, as they did in England before the Reformation, and at such institutions Rasputin became a popular figure. At certain convents the mock-monk, with the connivance of the Pravoslavny Church, was eagerly entertained by the dissolute nuns, more especially at Novo Tchevkask, on the Don, as well as at Viatka, and at Saratov, in Kasan.

From the convent of Novo Dievichy (The Convent of the Virgins) near the last-mentioned town, a great place which overlooks the Volga half way to Wolgsk, some terrible scandals leaked out, when the Mother-Superior, probably to save herself from the public indignation, brought in four sturdy mujiks from the countryside, who pitched the "Saint" out into the road, and administered such a severe kicking that the "Holy Father"—as the Tsaritza afterwards called him—could only creep about in pain for many days after!

Two months later, according to a report countersigned by Paul Dragomrioff, superintendent of the Secret Police of Moscow—a screed which, being somewhat ill-written, is difficult of translation—Rasputin was in that city. I here quote from it:—

"Report of Ivan Obroutcheff, Police-agent, Number 1287, of the 2nd Division, Secret Police, stationed at Moscow. April 2nd:—

"According to instructions from Police Headquarters, I visited at orders of Superintendent Dragomrioff, Number 136, Tverskaia, next to Loukonture's papier-mache factory at 1:35 A.M. to-day. I there found in a carpeted but barely furnished room an assembly of the cult of the Naked Believers kneeling before the monk, Gregory Novikh. Twenty-eight persons, all being women, fourteen of them ladies of birth and education, were present, and as I entered with my eight assistants the 'holy man' stood at the lectern, reading passages from the Gospel of St. Luke, interspersed with his own exhortations of the trials of the flesh. The walls of the room were decorated with disgusting pictures of a nature which would shock the modesty of all but the *demi-monde*, while behind the monk Novikh hung a copy of the Holy Ikon of Novgorod.

"In accordance with instructions all present were arrested after they had dressed, and I ordered them to be conducted to the Central Police Bureau, where their names and addresses were taken, and they were interrogated singly. Most of the midnight worshippers expressed indignation, and more especially the 'Saint' Rasputin, who demanded in the name of the Tsar that he might telegraph to the Empress. My superior officer, Nemiloff, Chief of Secret Police of Moscow, could not deny him this privilege. The result has been that by eleven o'clock next day an order came from the Tsar for the release of all the prisoners, and orders that no facts should be permitted to appear in the Press. Grichka has left for the capital by the 4:15 express this afternoon.

Signed: Ivan Obroutcheff

The report above quoted shows Rasputin in the early stages of his shameless debauchery. In London we have had the notorious Swami, with her male accomplice, practising similar acts upon innocent girls, but in Moscow the drunken and verminous monk with his hair-shirt, a rope around his waist and sandals upon his bulging feet, had attracted a select *coterie* of society women, daughters and wives of some of the greatest nobles of Russia, who, in secret and with gold in their hands, vowed themselves as docile followers of this Siberian fisherman whom nature had equipped as a satyr of such a type that happily none has ever been known in Britain in all its glorious years of history.

I readily admit that the career of Grichka, the man whose name the Censor does not allow to be mentioned, the sinister power that later on so suddenly appeared behind the Russian throne and whose true story I am here revealing, will appear incredible to my readers. I have written many works of fiction which some, of you may have read. But no work of mine has ever contained facts so extraordinary as the real life of this unwashed charlatan who, under the active protection of his debauched Church—and I write here with a true and reverent sense of our Christian religion—succeeded in establishing himself in the apartments of the favourite lady-in-waiting upon the Empress, and further, to teach his horrible "religion" to the innocent daughters of the Tsar in turn!

Much has already appeared in the newspapers regarding the sturdy unkempt rogue, but the greater part of it has emanated from the brains of writers who have not had access to official documents.

In these present articles my intention is to tell the British public the bare unvarnished truth culled from documentary evidence at my disposal, and to leave them to form their own conclusions. Russia, our great Ally, is, alas, still mysterious and much behind the times. True, she has a press, a Duma, and many modern social institutions. Yet her civilisation is only upon the surface. The Empire is, unfortunately, still the same as England was under the Tudors, an underworld of profligacy, plotting, and strange superstitions. The latter have, of course, been recently revived in London, as is proved by the prosecution of the fortune-tellers of Regent Street and St. John's Wood. Again, were not the scandals of the "Abode of Love" much the same as that of Rasputin's dozen-wived harem which he established in Pokrovsky?

The criminal records of Holy Russia teem with amazing stories of this "holy" scoundrel who from a drunken Siberian fisherman rose, by erotic suggestion, to become the greatest consolation to the Empress, and the lever by which "Nikki the Autocrat" was flung from his throne.

I remember how, when in Sofia, in the pre-war days with Sir George Buchanan, then our Minister to Bulgaria, and now ambassador to Russia, a cultured and clever diplomat to whom Great Britain owes more than she can ever know, and hence cannot acknowledge, we discussed the mystery of Russia and of the subtle influences near the Throne.

Little did either of us dream that he would now be ambassador to the Russian Court, and I would be writing this exposure of the evil life of the blasphemous satyr Rasputin.

The cult established by the pilgrimages of this illiterate peasant grew apace. The "holy father" whose disgraceful past is recorded in the police *dossiers* at Tyumen and Tobolsk had, by his astounding power of hypnotism, gathered around him a crowd of "Sister-disciples," mostly of the upper and leisured classes, to whom the new religion of nature strongly appealed.

Upon his constant pilgrimages to Jaroslav, Vologda, Vitebsk, Orel and other places, he made converts everywhere. He declared that no woman could obtain favour of the Almighty without first committing sexual sin, because that sin was the one which was forgiven above all others. At his weekly seances at which, strange to say, the highest born ladies in the Empire attended in secret, the most disgraceful scenes were witnessed, the dirty unwashed monk, a most repellent creature to all save his "disciples," acting as the high-priest of this erotic sisterhood.

Soon the disgusting rogue began to perform "miracles." Into his confidence he took a young man named Ilya Kousmitch—who, be it said, afterwards made certain statements to those who at last meted out justice and who provided me with certain details—and with the young fellow's connivance he succeeded in bamboozling a number of perfectly respectable and honest women in Petrograd, as well as in Moscow and Kiev, where he effected some really mysterious "cures."

In one instance at the house of a certain Madame Litvinoff, in the Sergiyevskaya, the most fashionable quarter of Petrograd, the man known as "the Stareb," or "Grichka," held a select meeting of his followers. The shameless charlatan treated the ladies who had assembled to worship him and to contribute lavishly to his imaginary charities, with the greatest disdain and most brutal contempt. This man, guilty of the most appalling vices, addressed them as usual in a strange illiterate jumble, urging them to follow the new religion which he called "the trial of the flesh," interspersing his remarks with occult jargon from works upon black magic, interlarded with those self-same scriptural quotations which will be found marked in that big Bible used by the Swami and her fellow-criminal—a volume now preserved in the Black Museum at Scotland Yard.

One of the women present, a certain Baroness Korotki, was suffering from acute rheumatism. The "Saint" placed his hands upon her, looked into her eyes with that intense unwavering stare of his, uttered some strange incantation, and lo! the pains left her, and she declared herself healed! The effect was electrical. Others declared themselves suffering from various imaginary maladies, and after performing certain rites as laid down by the "Holy Father," he laid hands upon them one after the other, and hypnotised them into a belief that they were cured.

Next day reports of these amazing "cures" ran like wildfire through Petrograd, and the superstitious lower-classes were at once seized by a belief that the Saint "Grichka," head of the fast-growing organisation of thinly disguised sensuality, was really a holy man and could work miracles. Around him crowded the halt and maimed and the blind, and aided by his accomplice Ilya Kousmitch, he not only pretended to effect cures, but succeeded in making many more converts among the lower-class women by declaring, as he had told the society dames, that there was in him a portion of the Divine with whom, as he put it, "all that would be saved must be one in the flesh and in the spirit!"

At one of his reunions, held a week or so later at Madame Litvinoff's, there attended Madame Vyrubova, the handsome leading lady-in-waiting at Court, and the chamber-confidante of both Tsar and Tsaritza. Like the others, this intriguing woman at once fell beneath the mock-monk's inexplicable spell. His new religion of the flesh appealed to her erotic temperament, and she at once became one of his most passionate devotees, a few days later introducing him at Court with astonishing result.

The subtle intrigues of Madame Vyrubova were many.

As chamber-confidante of both Emperor and Empress she had for a long time assisted in the spiritualistic seances which were given in private at Tsarskoe-Selo by a Russian monk named Helidor and his French friend, known as "Philippe." The young Tsarevitch was in a state of fast-declining health, and Helidor, as a "holy man," had, at Madame's suggestion, been called in to pray for him. Spiritualistic practices followed in strictest secrecy, and the credulous Empress first believed that the "holy man's" dealings with the unseen were resulting in a beneficial effect upon the weakly lad.

At last, however, owing to. Court intrigue, Helidor fell out of favour. It was just after this when Anna Vyrubova first met and fell beneath the evil influence of Rasputin. Grichka was a "miracle-worker," and might, she thought, perhaps restore the Tsarevitch to health! She knew that the Empress, a shallow-minded, ephemeral woman, lived for one object alone, namely, to secure for her son the crown of Romanoff. But the physicians gave but little hope of this. In a year—perhaps before—he must die, they had whispered. Helidor had been dismissed. Would Rasputin be more successful?

Madame sought out the charlatan who was busy with many "cures," and suggested that he should accompany her to the Palace, but with lordly disdain the drunken fisherman from Pokrovsky declared that to him all men and women were equal.

To a friend, a certain Madame Kovalenko, wife of one of the high Court officials, Madame Vyrubova described this interview. It took place in Petrograd at the house of a rich merchant living in the Tavritsheskaya, opposite the gardens. When the lady-in-waiting, who had, like so many others, fallen beneath his spell, had made the suggestion that the master should be introduced to the Court circle, he placed his left hand behind his back, a favourite attitude of his, drew himself up and began to address her in that strange jargon which she hardly understood—quotations from the "Lives of the Saints" jumbled up with lewd suggestions, high phrases, and meaningless sentences. As conclusion to this speech, however, the wily fellow added:

"I care nothing for the rulers of earth, but only for the Ruler of Heaven, who has bestowed upon me His blessing, and has led me into the path of honour, righteousness and peace. The rulers, of earth worship in their chapels and their tinsel cathedrals, but I worship everywhere, in the air, in the woods, in the streets, and you, lady, worship with me in body and in soul." And he raised his cold eyes upward, his right hand with its bulgy joints and broken dirty finger nails being placed across his breast. Then he sighed, as he added: "Ah! you do not yet understand! God has placed within me the power to smite—as well as to heal."

Madame Vyrubova, fascinated by his strange hypnotic glance, fell upon her knees before the "Saint," and kissing his bulgy unclean hand begged of him again and again to see the Empress.

But the artful scoundrel remained obdurate. He knew of Helidor's disgrace, and did not intend to hold himself at all cheaply.

The result was that Madame Vyrubova sought him next day and, handed him an autograph note from the Empress inviting him to come to the Winter Palace and see the Grand Duke Alexis. He read it, secretly much gratified, for he knew that not only had his latest devotee prevailed upon the Empress to seek the aid of another Russian monk to succeed the degraded Helidor, but that the Pravoslavny Church, the most powerful influence of State governance, had also been responsible for the invitation he held within his dirty fingers.

From that moment Rasputin's power became assured—a power he wielded for evil from that hour until the day of his well-deserved end.

When that grey afternoon the unkempt libertine was introduced to the small white-and-gold private salon of the Empress, which overlooks the gardens and the Neva on the northern wing of the palace, the Princess Obolensky, Princess Orbeliani and Countess Hendrikoff, maids-of-honour, were with Her Majesty, curious to see what manner of man it was who could perform miracles, and whom so many of the Society women in Petrograd and Moscow now acknowledged and addressed as "Master."

Upon the threshold the mock-monk halted, and in that dramatic attitude, struck in order to impress his hearers, he stood with his left arm behind him, erect, with his unkempt head thrown back, his face stern and relentless, his grey eyes sharp and piercing.

For some moments he remained there in statuesque silence, well-knowing how women were impressed by that pose. The hypnotism of those grey eyes few of the opposite sex could withstand. His conquests, or "conversions" as he termed them—were in every direction, and in every city. The Cult of the Naked Believers had rapidly spread everywhere. He was besieged by female disciples eager to hold meetings, for without the actual presence of the Saint true worship of the erotic could not take place.

"Great Lady!" he exclaimed at last in his deep, heavy voice, still that of the Siberian mujik, "you desire me here? I have come!"

The Empress rose and stretching out her hand eagerly welcomed the unholy charlatan into the Court circle, and half-an-hour later introduced him to fully a dozen of the highest-born women of the Empire, all of whom were at once impressed by his affected piety and humility. But a "dark force" had now entered the very heart of Russia, and later that afternoon, in a luxuriously furnished bedroom the miracle-worker was shown the poor little Heir to the Throne lying upon his sick couch, he placed hands upon him, and Her Majesty herself fell victim to that strange spell which other women had found so indescribable and so inexplicable.

"I will cure your son," said Rasputin slowly, after he had knelt beside him and looked long and earnestly into his eyes without uttering a word.

Madame Vyrubova was present and exchanged glances of relief with the Empress. To the latter, easily impressionable as she was, though all believed her to be a staid mother of a family, Rasputin became at once a Saint, a Divine agent, a miraculous guide. He had cured the poor; why could he not, if he willed it, cure her son?

Then in the days that followed "incidents" occurred in the Palace. At select assemblies of one or two of the Empress's confidantes—parties, of course, arranged by Madame Vyrubova, Rasputin expounded his shameless "religion." His jargon, the jumbled phrases of an illiterate peasant who knew not the meaning of what he uttered, his exhortations to commit sin so that it might be forgiven, his declaration of self-divinity, and his odds and ends of scripture mixed with the foulest vocabulary of Russian, was listened to with bated breath. Why?

Because, strange though it may seem, the health of the young Grand Duke Alexis had taken a sudden turn for the better. Even his physicians were compelled to acknowledge it!

Whether the latter were in any way under the influence of Rasputin by means of money-payment—for the fellow had by this time acquired a considerable fortune from his dupes—has not yet been ascertained. One thing, however, is shown in the documents before me, namely, that the mock-monk's "miracles" were often effected by means of secret drugs of which he had quite a curious extensive knowledge. How this was acquired is again a mystery, save that he was very friendly with a certain student of Chinese and Thibetan medicine, named Badmayeff, and that this person regularly furnished him at high prices with certain little-known drugs from the Far East.

With the gradual improvement of the health of the poor little Grand Duke, Rasputin's ascendancy over the Empress rapidly increased. He had been introduced to the Emperor, who, though regarding him with askance, tolerated him merely because his beloved son was improving beneath his daily prayerful treatment. Meanwhile, the canker-worm of Rasputin's religion had, fostered by the Empress's favourite lady-in-waiting, entered into the Court circle, and many secret meetings were held in the Palace where under the pseudo-religious cloak certain ladies of the Russian Court became devotees of the "Holy Father," and practised abominations absolutely incredible.

Official reports contain both dates and names of those who gave themselves into the unscrupulous hands of this man who claimed the Divine right and thus worshipped as "Believers."

Rasputin was too clever a scoundrel to allow matters to proceed quite smoothly. Several chance conversations with the Emperor and with Stolypin convinced him that he might ultimately share the same obscurity as Helidor. He therefore one day pretended to be offended at some words of the Empress—whom he now addressed by the familiar terms of "thee" and "thou" which he used to his disciples, though even the Grand Dukes and Duchesses would have hesitated so to address the Empress—and after a dramatic farewell, he took himself off to the wonderful and luxurious monastery which, according to his statement to the Empress, he had built at his native Pokrovsky with the money he had collected upon his various pilgrimages.

To the female section of Petrograd society he had been never tired of describing the beauties of this monastery where his fellow-monks lived a life of severe asceticism and constant prayer, therefore at his sudden resolve to leave, the capital—or the better-class women of it—grew tearful and the Empress most of all.

Within four days of his departure for Siberia the little Tsarevitch was taken suddenly ill, and the Empress, beside herself at having expressed any words of doubt concerning the unkempt Saint who had so entirely entered into her life, telegraphed wildly to him. This message, since unearthed by the Revolutionary Party, which ran as follows:—

"I cannot bear your absence. Life is so grey and hopeless without you, my dear comforter, my master. Alexis has been taken ill. Do not take any notice of Kokovtsov. He is responsible for my hasty words to you and shall suffer for it. Forgive me. Return—for my sake and for the life of Alexis.

Alec

But the crafty mujik was not to be thus entrapped. He had been guest of the Minister Kokovtsov, a week before, and his host and his friends had made him roaring drunk. In his cups he had made certain revelations. What they were the Saint could not recollect. Hence he had absented himself from Court, in order to maintain his Divine dignity—and to plot further.

At this point it is necessary to make a critical remark.

For two years Rasputin had been speaking of his monastery at Pokrovsky. In the salons and boudoirs of Moscow and Kiev as well as in

Petrograd, society spoke of the institute, discussed it and declared that indeed Grichka was a holy man. The Metropolitan with his rich robes and jewels, and all the bishops were as common clay in comparison with the "Holy Father" who could cure by the laying-on of hands, who walked in humility and who devoted himself to good works. Curiously enough it had occurred to nobody, not even to the ever-ubiquitous police of Petrograd, to investigate the story told by Rasputin regarding his monastery at far-off Pokrovsky.

The world of Russia did not, of course, know that in that Siberian village there still lived Rasputin's peasant-wife with her children, or that his life had been so evil, a career of drink and profligacy which even in Siberia stood out in letters of scarlet in the police *dossiers* of Tobolsk. It, however, remained for a female spy of the Revolutionary Party—a certain lady named Vera Aliyeff, from whose report I am writing—to travel to that sordid Siberian village and watch the Court charlatan in his home. I may here say that to the untiring efforts of Mademoiselle Aliyeff is in a great measure due the downfall and assassination of the terribly sinister influence which cost the Tsar Nicholas his throne, and hundreds of women their good name—as I shall afterwards show.

But to relate matters in their proper sequence as history I may here quote from the report of this patriotic woman-revolutionary who travelled to Rasputin's home in disguise, because he knew her, and as she was good-looking, he had already endeavoured to induce her to join the Cult of the Naked Believers. She reports:—

"I found the great monastery of Pokrovsky to be a dirty repellent hamlet of mujiks of the worst and most illiterate type. There was no trace of the marble palace which Rasputin had described as having erected as the main building of the monastery. The latter was, I found, a large, cheaply built, ordinary-looking house, three rooms of which were given up to the 'Saint's' peasant-wife, his son Dmitri and the younger of his two daughters, while in the other part of the house lived twelve women of varying ages—the youngest being sixteen—who were his fascinated devotees and who had given up their lives in Europe to enter the seclusion of that sordid home and become his spiritual brides."

Here Mademoiselle Aliyeff had an interview with the woman Guseva, and later on after an inspection of the police records at Tobolsk and Tyumen, she returned to Petrograd and reported the result of her visit to the Right Party in the Duma.

WILLIAM LE QUEUX

Meanwhile, the Empress and also her favourite lady-in-waiting telegraphed to Rasputin urgently imploring him to return to Petrograd. But the verminous libertine was in too comfortable quarters with his dozen devotees to stir out far from his nest, and while going about the village standing drinks to all and sundry and ingratiating himself everywhere, he at the same time treated his old and ugly wife with brutal unconcern, and refused even to reply to the Imperial demand.

At last he grew weary of his retirement—for, truth to tell, he usually retired there whenever he disappeared upon his many pretended pilgrimages in Russia—whereupon he one day sent a telegram to the Empress saying that he had at last been directed by a Divine call to again return to the bedside of the Tsarevitch. This message was received with the greatest joy at Tsarskoe-Selo, where it set a-flutter hearts in which beat the noblest blood of Russia.

"The Holy Father is on his way back to us!" Such was the message whispered along the long stone corridors of the Winter Palace, the many windows of which look out upon the grey Neva. The Empress went to her son's bedroom and told him the glad news, laying a tender hand upon the poor lad's brow.

And Madame Vyrubova meeting the Emperor as he came out of his private cabinet chatting with the Duke of Mecklenburg-Strelitz and the Minister Protopopoff, whispered the news into his ear.

The Tsar smiled happily. Little did His Majesty dream that by that return of the unwashed scoundrel whom the most delicately nurtured women worshipped, he was doomed to lose his throne.

On Rasputin's arrival some intensely dramatic scenes ensued—scenes that would be deemed fantastic if any modern novelist had dared to describe them even as fiction.

But from these voluminous reports and the *dossier* before me I shall attempt to describe them.

II

Scandals at the Winter Palace

The rascalities of Rasputin were unparalleled, even in Russia.

The mock-monk, much against his will, returned to the Winter Palace where the Court had gone for a few days and only because of the Divine call, as he pretended. He treated the distracted Tsaritza with utter disdain when early one wintry morning he drove in from the Dvortsovy Square, passed the Palace Guards, and ascended the wide black-and-white marble staircase of the Great Hall, where she stood eager to receive him.

"Ah! Forgive me! Forgive me, my Master!" implored the Empress in a low agonised tone. "I was thoughtless and foolish."

"Take me to Alexis," said the charlatan roughly interrupting her. "He is ill—very ill—and God has sent me to him."

Eagerly the Empress conducted him to the bedside of her son, the little Tsarevitch. Madame Vyrubova, the mistress of Rasputin, was awaiting him, together with two nurses and a physician named Letchitzki.

With rough deep-voiced dismissal the unkempt profligate sent everyone from the room, including the Empress herself. He wished to pray by the sick lad's bedside, he explained.

This he did, Madame Vyrubova alone remaining. When the door was closed the blasphemous rascal quickly bent over the Heir to ascertain that he was sleeping, then he raised his own dirty hands for Madame to kiss, crossing himself at the same time, and whispering "The drug? It seems to have acted well—eh? Where is it?" She slipped a tiny green-glass phial from her cream silk blouse and handed it to him, saying: "Yes, Badmayeff was right! Each time I gave it to him in his milk, he grew worse."

"Ah!" laughed the verminous fellow, his sensuous face bearded and blotchy with drink. "Now that I have returned Divine Providence will restore him. He will not get his six drops each day!" The dastardly charlatan and poisoner of Russia's heir concealed the Thibetan drug in the folds of his ample habit, and whispering in his rough uncouth peasant way, "Now let the fools in again!" he threw himself upon his knees by the bedside commencing a fervent prayer.

"O God—the Great! the Merciful! the Giver of all Bounties, the Creator, and the Death-giver—the Maker of Kings and the Destroyer of Nations—to Thee we pray—and of Thee we ask—"

And as he uttered those blasphemous words the favourite lady-in-waiting opened the long white-and-gold door to admit the Imperial mother of the poor half-conscious elder son of the great House of Romanoff—the boy whose life was being trifled with by the administration of those pernicious drugs which, at any moment, when "Rasputin" willed, might cause death from haemorrhage.

The fellow Novikh, the low-born thief and blackmailer from the far-off wilds of Siberia, had planted himself in the Winter Palace as a divinity to be worshipped. The Court circle of silly women in search of sensation, and headed by the Empress herself, had fallen entirely beneath his baneful influence, believing that only by first practising his disgusting rites could they offer prayers to the Almighty. Another of the Empress's intimates who had joined the Palace circle of Believers was Countess Ignatieff, who had also become a most devout follower of Rasputin and who exerted all her great influence in officialdom for his benefit and protection.

War had broken out, and while the newspapers of the Allies were full of Russia's greatness and the irresistible power of her military "steamroller," the world was in utter ignorance that the Empress was actually educating her own daughters to enter the secret cult of the "Believers," a suggestion which they eventually obeyed! Such was the truly horrible state of affairs at Court. Thus in a few brief months that unmasked thief whom the workers of Petrograd contemptuously called "Grichka," and whose very name Rasputin meant "the ne'er-do-well" had, by posing as a holy man, and a worker of mock "miracles," become a power supreme at Court.

Daily at eleven each morning this verminous libertine, whose weekly reunions were in reality orgies as disgraceful as any organised by the Imperial satyr Tiberius, knelt at the bedside of the poor little Tsarevitch to drone his blasphemous appeals to God, while the Empress, always present, knelt humbly in a corner listening to that jumble of exhortations, threats, and amazing assertions of his own divine right as high-priest of the Believers. The Empress had fallen completely beneath the hypnotism of the grey steely eyes, the hard sphinx-like countenance that never smiled, and those long dirty knotted fingers, the nails of which were never cleaned. To her, filth, both moral and personal, was synonymous with godliness.

Then, after each prayer, Madame Vyrubova would assist the mock-monk to rise and declare—

"The Holy Father is, alas! tired," and then lead him off into the adjoining ante-room overlooking the Neva where a silk-stockinged flunkey stood ready to serve the scoundrel with his usual bottle of Heidsieck monopole—the entire contents of which he would quickly empty and smack his lips over in true peasant manner.

Mademoiselle Sophie Tutcheff, governess of the Tsar's daughters, very quickly perceived a change in the demeanour of her charges. They were no longer the charming ingenuous girls they were before. She had overheard whispered conversations between the Grand Duchess Tatiana and her sister, Marie. Rasputin, moreover, had now been given luxurious apartments in the Palace, close to the rooms occupied by Madame Vyrubova, and each day he came to the schoolroom in which the three younger Princesses, Tatiana, Marie and Anastasia were prosecuting their studies.

It did not take Mademoiselle Tutcheff long to discern the true state of affairs. The monk one day used the most lewd language while chatting with the three young Grand Duchesses, whereupon Mademoiselle, who belonged to one of the highest families in Russia, went off to the Empress in disgust and indignation. Her protests were, as may be imagined, met with withering scorn.

"I am Empress and the Holy Father is our guest in the Palace," exclaimed the Tsaritza, who was taking tea with two ladies of the Court who were her fellow-Believers. "What you have said is an insult to him. You are dismissed in disgrace."

And an hour later poor Mademoiselle left the Palace without her pupils being allowed to bid her farewell.

This, however, was but one illustration of the power which the rascally ex-highwayman had secured over the Imperial Court, and hence over the great Russian Empire itself. His influence was more powerful than that of all the Grand Dukes, the Council of the Empire, and the Council of Ministers put together. True, His Majesty was Tsar, but Gregory Rasputin was equally powerful, if not more so, because of his innate craftiness, his pseudo-divinity, his mock miracles, and the support he received from a certain section of the Church.

Possessed of the curious cunning of the erotic criminal lunatic, Rasputin never allowed matters to run calmly for very long. He was much too clever for that, well knowing, that while Protopopoff,

Minister of the Interior was his friend, he had as powerful enemies, both Stolypin and Miliukoff—who, later on, became Minister for Foreign Affairs. Both the latter he feared, as well as the Grand Duke Nicholas Michailovitch.

The latter had secretly learnt much concerning the ex-thief of the far-off Siberian village—more, indeed, than Rasputin had ever dreamed. One day, a week after the departure of Mademoiselle Sophie Tutcheff, the Grand Duke attended a great reception at the Winter Palace. The usual brilliant throng had assembled; the usual Imperial procession had taken place down the great Nicholas Hall, that famous salon wherein three thousand people can dance at one time—the salon the walls of which are adorned with golden plates, and where on the night of a Court ball the assembly is indeed a gorgeous one of stars, medals, exquisite dresses and brilliant uniforms. Though Russia was at war, the Empress had given the ball, and all Russian Court Society had assembled.

Among the throng were two men the Bishop Teofan, of the Pravoslavny Church, and with him the monk, silent and unbending, upon whom the eyes of all the women were turned. Naturally there were many strange whisperings among those who were "Believers" and those who had not been initiated into the cult of the "Sister-disciples," whispers among the old and young—whispers which were not meant for any male ear.

Bishop and monk passed down the great ballroom, through the beautiful winter-garden beyond, where many men and women were chatting beneath the palms, and then into the Oriental gallery, a place decorated with those engraved golden and silver plates which Catherine the Great received with bread and salt from those who came to do her homage.

Thence the pair disappeared into one of the side rooms to what is known as the Jordan Entrance.

A tall, bald-headed man with heavy brow, moustache, small round beard, and wearing a brilliant white uniform with many decorations had followed the pair from the ball-room. With him walked a young, clean-shaven, dark-haired man in uniform, erect and determined.

The elder was the Grand Duke Nicholas Michailovitch, the younger the Grand Duke Dmitri Pavlovitch.

They entered the small room unceremoniously, and confronted the illiterate Bishop and the peasant charlatan.

"We have come to turn you out of the Palace!" exclaimed the elder man firmly. "Your presence is obnoxious to us, especially the charlatan of Pokrovsky. We are Grand Dukes of Russia, and we have no intention to mix with convicted thieves and beguilers of women! Come!" His Imperial Highness cried, "Go! You are not wanted here!"

"And pray by what right do you speak thus?" asked the Starets with offensive insolence.

"By the right of my position," was the Grand Duke's reply.

In response, Rasputin spat upon the pale blue carpet in defiance.

In a moment the young Grand Duke Dmitri Pavlovitch, an athletic young officer who had only the day before returned from the German Front where he had been with von Rennenkampf, took the dirty monk by the scruff of his neck and flung him outside into the big marble hall, administering to him a severe kick in the presence of a dozen of the astonished Palace guards.

"Put this scoundrel outside!" he commanded the men, and two minutes later, Rasputin, with his dirty black habit badly torn, found himself flung down the steps headlong into the snow.

Meanwhile the Grand Duke Nicholas had administered to the dissolute Bishop—whose sister, by the way, was one of Rasputin's "spiritual brides" at his monastery, or harem, at Pokrovsky—a very severe castigation and with his own hands had torn the big crucifix from his neck and cast it across the room.

Then, when at last the Bishop emerged into the Hall, he shared, at the Grand Duke's order, the same indignity that had befallen the dissolute blackguard whom the Empress caressed and called her "Holy Father."

Of this episode Rasputin made no mention to Her Majesty. It, however, caused him considerable misgivings and before morning he had decided upon a dramatic course of action.

Next afternoon, a Wednesday, was the day fixed for the usual performance of the bi-weekly secret rites. He took luncheon with the Emperor and Empress in their private apartments, Madame Vyrubova alone being the only other person at table.

Suddenly the monk who had been talking with the Emperor, using his uncouth Siberian expressions, and even eating with his fingers, clasped his knotted, peasant fingers together and turning to the Empress, announced:

"To-night, Great Lady, I go upon a pilgrimage. Divine God has called me to Moscow, where work there awaits me. I know not what it is, but when I arrive there I shall receive His divine direction. Alexis will be well in my absence, and will improve, for twice each day he will have my prayers. God has called me—I cannot remain."

"Not even this afternoon?" gasped the unnerved hysterical woman who was Empress of Russia in this our Twentieth Century.

"No. I must take leave of you, great lady, to obey the call," was his deep answer.

And by that night's express he left in a luxurious sleeping-berth for Moscow where, truth to tell, the Countess Ignatieff was awaiting him.

The only "call" the licentious blackguard had received was the news that two very prepossessing young girls, named Vera and Xenie, daughters of the late Baroness Koulomzine, of Moscow, had expressed their desire to Countess Ignatieff to join the secret cult. The Countess had shown him their photographs and the libertine, in pretence of performing a pilgrimage, travelled to Moscow in order to initiate them. Next day, at the Convent of the Ascension, where the libertine had spent the night, he interviewed the two young gentlewomen. Before an ikon with flowers upon the altar and in the presence of the Lady-Superior, he exorcised their sins according to his prescribed rite.

It was a strange scene. The penitents in the dimly-lit chapel each touched their forehead and breast with thumb and forefinger, gazing immobile and fascinated at the miracle-working "Master," their lips moving in proper response to the prayers of the Heaven-sent confessor.

At what subsequently transpired I can only hint. According to the official report before me the girls confessed to two officers, their half-brothers, that after the benediction the verminous monk induced them both to go to the Turkish baths together, for "purification" as he put it.

Well, the mock-monk found himself under arrest, and only by the most strenuous efforts of the Countess Ignatieff was he released, after spending forty hours in a cell.

But Rasputin merely smiled. He knew his own power. Next day he returned to Petrograd, and within twelve hours of his arrival Plestcheff, Chief of Police of Moscow, had, at the instance of the Empress, been relieved of his post in disgrace.

Rasputin's exploits in Moscow brought him very nearly to disaster.

Master-criminal that he was and as my intention is to show, he calmly reviewed his position, and saw that by cleverly playing his cards—now that the Empress and her easily gulled Court had become so completely enthralled by his "wonder-working"—he might assume his own position as the most powerful man in the Empire.

His personal magnetism is indisputable. I can personally vouch for that. On the occasion when I met him in that grey cold repellent village on the Arctic shore, I myself felt that there was something strangely indescribable, something entirely uncanny about the fellow. Those grey eyes were such as I had never before seen in all my long cosmopolitan experience. In those moments when we had exchanged greetings and bowed to each other he seemed to hold me beneath a weird curious spell. He was demon rather than man. Therefore I can quite conceive that the ordinary Russian woman of any class would easily succumb to his blasphemous advances and his assertions that he was possessed of a divinity as the deliverer of Russia. Within the Russian soul, two centuries behind the times, of to-day, mysticism is still innate, and the mock-monk had already proved up to the hilt to his own complete satisfaction that, by pretending to fast, yet having a good square meal in secret; by pretending to make pilgrimages—but really throwing off his monkish "habits" and as a gay man about town taking a joy-ride in a motor car—and by crossing himself continuously and bowing low before every ikon at which he secretly sneered, he could gull the average woman whether she wore pearls or tended the pigs.

Rasputin, a low-born immoral brute, by reason of the discovery of his own hypnotic powers, treated womenkind with the most supreme and utter contempt, and it seems that while clearly masquerading beneath that cloak of extreme piety and aided by his gardener-friend, the Bishop Teofan—a fellow-adventurer from Pokrovsky—he resolved after his Moscow adventure, to make a bold bid for further power.

Most men in such circumstances as these would have been both cowed and careful. Against him he had Stolypin, at that moment one of the most powerful men in the Empire, as well as the Grand Dukes Nicholas and Dmitri Pavlovitch, M. Gutchkoff—a bearded man in gold pince-nez with whom I had had before the war many interesting chats in Paris and in Petrograd, and who subsequently became Minister of War and Marine—M. Miliukoff, the whole-hearted Deputy for Petrograd in the Duma, and what was far more serious, he had fifty or more wildly irate husbands and fathers, all eager and anxious to bring about the scoundrel's downfall.

Traps were laid for him, but, with the amazing cunning of the erotic lunatic, he eluded them all. Back in Petrograd, in the salons of the highest in the Empire, he lived in luxury, with cars always at his disposal. The "Holy Father" who had his own suite in the private apartments of the Imperial family was welcomed everywhere he deigned to go. His creature, Ilya Kousmitch, warned him of the pitfalls that were being set. Even his dissolute crony the Bishop Teofan—whom, through the Empress, he had himself created—grew grave. But the "Saint" merely bit his dirty finger nails, as is the habit of the Siberian peasant, and replied:

"Gregory Novikh has been sent to Russia by Divine Providence. He has no fear!"

Soon after his narrow escape in Moscow he received a letter from the father of the two young girls who had so completely fallen beneath his pious blandishments—a letter in which the angry father declared that he would shoot him at sight.

To that letter Rasputin, with the overbearing impudence of one who smoked and spat upon the carpet actually in the Empress's presence, and, who had the audacity to prompt the Tsar in making his appointments and dealing with the affairs of State, replied by telegram—a message still upon record—sent over the private wire from the Winter Palace:

"Shoot—and God will reward your daughters bountifully.

Gregory

Though Rasputin presented a remarkably calm exterior, he no doubt, was much perturbed by that threat. A single false step would certainly land him either in oblivion or in prison. But criminal lunatics of his sort are notoriously clever and astute. "Jack-the-Ripper" was of exactly similar type, and he defied the whole detective police of the world.

The Secret Police of Russia, the wiles of which have been so vaunted by the modern novelist, were as childish idiots when their brains became pitted against those of the uncouth Siberian peasant, who, calling himself a "saint," could induce every silly woman to follow his immoral directions.

Just then the Empress, whose shallow impressionable mind led her to adopt any new craze, and to seek any new sensation, met a person in whom she indiscreetly placed her trust—a treacherous, long-bearded political adventurer, named Boris Sturmer. This man was a boon companion of the "Saint" in his debaucheries in the midnight wilds of Petrograd, for Rasputin, when believed to be absent for a week of prayer and self-denial, usually bathed himself, and wearing a well-cut evening-suit plunged into the gay midnight life at the Old Donon, the Belle Vue, or the Bouffes, on the Fontanka. Thus Boris Sturmer, a strong pro-German who had many family connections with the enemy—and the bosom friend of Rasputin—actually became Prime Minister of Russia, such being the mock-monk's astounding influence over the Imperial Autocrat, whose wife and family were, alas! as but clay within his filthy hands.

This latest triumph proved conclusively to Rasputin that his power was as great as that of the Emperor—indeed, to certain of his intimates he used laughingly to declare himself to be the uncrowned Tsar!

"I live in the Palace," he would declare. "The Empress does my bidding; her daughters are as my children; the Court bows to me; Nikki only smiles as an idiot—therefore, am I not the real Emperor of Russia?"

Discovering his own overwhelming influence this sinister favourite of both Tsar and Tsaritza suddenly resolved upon a further move, the cleverness of which was indeed well within keeping with his marvellously astute reasoning. He decided not to be dependent upon the charity of the Imperial pair, whom the Bishop Teofan had one day declared kept him in the Winter Palace as a tame saint. His friend's taunt stung him to the quick.

In consequence, he took a luxurious house in the Gorokhovaya, just beyond the Moyka, and close to the Palace, and while still retaining his apartments in the Palace, he lived mostly in his new abode, where in future he announced that the bi-weekly meeting of his disciples for prayer and consolation would be held.

Like wildfire the decision of the "wonder-worker" ran through the salons of Society. There was now a chance for others to enter the cult of the "Sister-disciples," and to become as one flesh with the Saint, and to be cured by Divine agency of any ill.

Hundreds of society women were frantically anxious to enter this new sisterhood.

His house was an expensive one, but only a few of the rooms were well furnished. The dining-room on the ground floor was a large rather bare-looking place, with cheap chairs set round and equally cheap tables of polished walnut. On the walls were portraits of the Tsar, the Tsaritza and himself. Upstairs was his study, a large luxurious apartment, and from it led the bedroom of the "holy" man, which even eclipsed the study in luxury. To this house the smart band of society converts who called themselves the "Sister-disciples" went regularly twice each week to hear the "miracle-worker" descant upon the beauties of his new religion.

Among the members of this degenerate group were:—the pretty fluffy-haired little Princess Boyarski, Madame Pistolcohrse, sister of Madame Vyrubova, a certain Countess Yepantchine, whose splendid house was in the Sergiyevskaya, the most fashionable quarter without equal in Petrograd, as well as the Grand Duchess Olga, daughter of the Tsaritza, and many others.

Though the blasphemous discourses were delivered and the disgusting secret rites practised twice each week at Rasputin's house, as well as also twice weekly in secret at Tsarskoe-Selo, many women seeking knowledge of the new religion—after having fallen beneath the spell of the mock-saint's eyes—went to the monk alone by appointment, and there had what the blackguard termed "private converse" with him in his upstairs study adjoining his luxurious sleeping apartment.

The uncouth peasant's actions, his open immorality, and the cold-blooded manner in which he turned wife from husband, and betrothed from her lover, had now become open gossip at the street corners. Whenever the mock-saint went forth in any car or carriage of his female admirers or of the Court, the people grinned and recognising the lady, would whisper—

"Look! Grichka has taken yet another bride!"

At some of the mysterious meetings Rasputin's old friend the dissolute Bishop Teofan was present, and on one occasion a dramatic incident occurred.

The little Princess Boyarski had apparently grown jealous of the "Saint" because he had paid too great attention to a new convert, a certain Mademoiselle Zernin, just turned twenty. High words arose in the select circle of worshippers, and the Bishop with his big golden cross on his breast endeavoured to quell the dispute. The Princess then turned furiously upon the Bishop, expressing the deepest resentment that he should have been admitted to their private conference at all, and vowed that she would use all her influence to get him turned out of the Church he had dishonoured.

Rasputin and his friend ridiculed her threats, but two days later both grew extremely uneasy, for Teofan was already extremely unpopular with the Court circle, and all were only too ready to effect his dismissal and disgrace. Indeed, forty-eight hours after the Princess had uttered those threats, she, with the Countess Kleinmichel, contrived to secure his expulsion from the Church. Only after Rasputin had threatened the Empress that he would leave Petrograd, and in that case the Tsarevitch would, he declared, die, that he secured the re-instalment of his fellow-criminal. Such was the scoundrel's influence at Court in these present war-days!

By various tricks, in which he was assisted by the young servant, the man Ilya, the charlatan still performed "miracles" upon the poor, which naturally caused his fame to spread all over Russia, while his sinister influence was now being felt both in the Orthodox Church, and in the conduct of the war. Contrary to what is generally supposed, he had never been ordained a priest, while he never attended church nor observed any of the forms of religious worship, save the immoral practices of his own invention.

He claimed a semi-divinity, and thus declared himself to be above all man-made laws.

In those scandalous discourses, in which he made use of the most erotic suggestions, he always urged his female devotees that only through his own body could they seek the protection and forgiveness of the Almighty.

"I show you the way!" he would constantly say as he stood with his hand behind his back, his other hand upon the Bible. "I am here to give you salvation."

Such was his power in ecclesiastical matters in Russia that the most lucrative posts in the Church were now filled by men who had paid him for their nominations, and he boasted that the Procurator of the Holy Synod was merely his puppet. From certain evidence before me I am inclined to believe this to be the truth, for some of the supposed "miracles" could never have been "worked" without the Procurator's connivance.

Daily, smart society women came to Rasputin's house for "private converse." Sometimes one of the circle of his elect would bring with her a young society girl who had heard vaguely of "the disciples," and whose curiosity was naturally aroused, to meet the wonderful wonder-worker. At others, women went alone. But in each case the result was the same.

One afternoon the young wife of the wealthy Count Ivanitski went there in secret, attired in one of her maid's dresses, so as to escape observation, passing through the servants' entrance. The Count, however, had heard whispers of this intended visit and, awaiting her return, followed her back to the Furshtavkaya, where they lived in a handsome house a few doors from the Liteyny Prospect. He then coolly called his servants and compelled her to confess before them all that had happened to her in Rasputin's house. Afterwards he drew a revolver and shot her dead. Then he walked out and gave himself up to the police. Within an hour news of the affair was brought to the Empress and to Rasputin, who were dining together in the Palace.

The monk made a sarcastic grimace when he heard of the murder of the woman who had that afternoon been his victim.

"Poor fool!" he exclaimed, his glass of wine in his hand. "The Countess had already become a devoted disciple."

But the Empress at once bestirred herself in fear of public indignation being aroused against the Holy Father, and telephoning to the Minister of the Interior, ordered the Count's immediate release.

On another occasion, a week later, a young lieutenant of cavalry named Olchowski, who had been with von Rennenkampf at Brest-Litovsk, had returned to Petrograd, being met at the railway station by his devoted young wife, a mere chit of a girl, the daughter of a Baroness living at Ostroff. They returned home together, whereupon somebody slipped into his hand an anonymous letter, stating that his pretty young wife Vera had become one of the "spiritual brides" who attended the bi-weekly meetings in the Gorokhovaya. The Lieutenant said nothing, but watching next afternoon he followed her to the meeting place of the "Naked Believers," and having satisfied himself that during his absence at the front his beloved wife had fallen beneath the "saint's" spell, he concealed himself in the porch of a neighbouring house until after the worshippers had all departed. Then Rasputin presently descended the steps to enter one of the Imperial carriages which had called for him as was usual each day.

In an instant the outraged husband, half-mad with fury, flung himself upon the "holy" libertine and plunged a long keen knife into his breast.

But Rasputin, whose strength was colossal, simply tossed his assailant away from him without a word, and entered the carriage.

Beneath his monkish hair-shirt he had for some time, at the Empress's urgent desire, worn another shirt which she had had specially made for him in Paris, as also for the Tsar—a light but most effective shirt of steel-mail.

III

How Rasputin Poisoned the Tsarevitch

The dark forces established so ingeniously by the Kaiser behind the Russian throne in April, 1914, had now become actively at work.

The small but all-powerful clique of which Rasputin was the head because he practically lived with the Imperial family and ate at their table—the little circle which the Russians called "The Camarilla"—were actively plotting for the betrayal of the Allies and a separate peace with Germany. Sturmer, the Austrian who had been pushed into the office of Prime Minister of Russia by his boon companion and fellow *bon-viveur*, the mock-monk of Pokrovsky, had already risen in power. The man whose long goatee-beard swept over the first button of his gorgeous uniform, all true loyal Russians in their unfortunate ignorance cheered wildly as he drove swiftly with the *pristyazhka*, or side-horse, along the Nevski, for he was believed to be "winning the war." Russia, alas! to-day knows that with German gold flowing freely into his pocket he was in secret doing all he could to prevent ministers arriving from Great Britain, and laughing up his sleeve at his success in ordering a mock-railway from Alexandrovsk to be built in order to connect Petrograd to an ice-free port—a line which subsequently had to be taken up and relaid!

Even our British journalists were cleverly bamboozled, for they returned from Russia and wrote in our newspapers of her coming great offensive, when they would sweep back the Kaiser's hordes and be into Berlin ere we should know it. In Petrograd one heard of Rasputin as the Shadowy Somebody. But most people declared that he was only a monk, a pious person whom silly women admired, as women so often admire a fashionable preacher even in our own country, and further because of "something," the Censor refused to allow his name to appear in any paper.

In Russia the censorship is full of vagaries. My own novels came under his ban twenty years ago, because as correspondent of *The Times* I had spoken some very plain truths in that journal. I remember well old Monsieur de Stael, then Russian ambassador in London and the cheeriest of good souls, laughing when I came back from Russia at my complaint regarding the censorship. "Why!" he said, "they censor my letters to my own daughter in Nijni! Please do not think any the less of Russia for that. You have been across the Empire, into Siberia, and surely you know how far we are behind the times!"

Russia had, after all, advanced but little in those intervening twenty years, though it has produced the rascal Rasputin.

That small circle of Germanophiles who met so frequently in secret at Rasputin's house in the Gorokhovaya—the scene of the bi-weekly orgies of the "Sister-Disciples"—though they were unaware of it were, with clever insinuation, being taught that a separate peace with Germany would be of greatest advantage to the Empire. They were hourly plotting, and the details of their conspiracies which have now come to light and are before me, documents in black and white, which had been carefully preserved by the monk, are truly amazing. Surely no novelist, living or dead, could have ever imagined a situation so astounding and yet so tragic, for the fate of one of the mightiest Imperial Houses of the modern world was now trembling in the balance.

That both the Prime Minister and his long-moustached sycophant Protopopoff, a political adventurer whose past is somewhat shady and obscure, were in daily consultation is plain from the reports of secret agents of the Revolutionists. The Duke Charles Michael, though heir to the Grand Duchy of Mecklenburg-Strelitz, had, as part of the German Emperor's subtle plot, become naturalised as a Russian three weeks before the declaration of war, and he, with the erotic scoundrel, was actively carding out Berlin's set programme in the salons of Tsarskoe-Selo.

"Grichka," the convicted thief from the far-off Siberian village, the man who had a dozen "spiritual brides" at Pokrovsky, uncouth, unlettered and unwashed, had by this time obtained such hypnotic hold upon the female portion of Petrograd society that when he deigned to accept an invitation to dine at the various palaces of the nobility he would eat from his plate with his dirty fingers and his female admirers actually licked them clean! This is absolute fact, vouched for by dozens of patriotic Russians whose names I could give.

It is contained in a plain report in cold unvarnished language in an official Russian report which is before me. Readers will, I believe, halt aghast. But such men have exercised the same powers over women—criminal lunatics always—through the long pages of history.

The heart of Russia was being eaten out by the German canker-worm. The high-born women of Petrograd were being used by Rasputin to play the Kaiser's game.

Outwardly Sturmer, Protopopoff, the Bishop Teofan, and their place-seeking friends were good loyal Russians bent upon winning the war. In secret, however, they were cleverly arranging to effect various crises. The supply of food was held up by a ring of those eager to profit, and the Empire became suddenly faced with semi-starvation, so that rioting ensued, and the police were kept busy. Then there succeeded serious railway troubles, congestion of traffic to and from the front, "faked" scandals of certain females whom the camarilla charged with giving away Russia's secrets to Germany. Some highly sensational trials followed, much perjured evidence was given, false reports of *agents provocateurs* produced, and several officers in high command who, though perfectly innocent, were actually condemned as traitors, merely because they had become obnoxious to Rasputin and his circle.

One day a sensational incident occurred when Rasputin visited the Ministry of the Interior, and sought the Adjunct-Minister Dzhunkovsky, who controlled the police of the Empire.

On being shown into his room the monk insolently demanded why he was being followed by police-agents, and why his friends who visited his house in the Gorokhovaya were being spied upon.

"My duty, my dear Father, is to know what is in progress in Petrograd," replied the Minister coldly.

"Are you not aware that I am immune from espionage by your confounded agents?" cried Rasputin in anger. "Are you in ignorance that my personal safety is in charge of the special Palace Police who are responsible for the safety of the Emperor?"

"My own actions are my own affair," was the chill reply—for truth to tell—the Revolutionists had already imparted to Dzhunkovsky certain evidence they had collected as to the traitorous conduct of the pseudo-monk and his traitorous friends.

High words arose. Grichka, losing his temper, made use of some very insulting remarks regarding the Minister's young wife, whereupon Dzhunkovsky sprang from his chair and promptly knocked down the "Saint."

An hour later Rasputin, with his eye bandaged, sat with the Empress in her room overlooking the Neva, and related how he had been assaulted by the Adjunct-Minister of the Interior, merely because he had expressed his unswerving loyalty to the throne. To the Empress the unwashed charlatan was as a holy man, and such insult caused her blood to boil with indignation.

The fellow knew quite well that no word uttered against himself was ever believed by either Emperor or Empress. They were all said to be stories invented by those jealous of the Saint's exalted position, and the wicked inventions of enemies of the Dynasty. Therefore, what happened was exactly what he expected. In a fury the neurotic Empress rose and went off to the Tsar who, then and there, signed a decree dismissing his loyal Adjunct-Minister from office, and appointing an obscure friend of Rasputin's in his place!

In that same week another incident occurred which caused the Saint no little apprehension. His Majesty had appointed Samarin as Procurator of the Holy Synod, an appointment which Rasputin knew might easily result in his own downfall. Samarin, an honest, upright man, was one of his most bitter enemies, for he knew the disgraceful past of both him and Teofan, and further he had gained accurate knowledge of which appointments of Bishops in the Pravoslavny Church had been the outcome of the ex-horse stealer's influence. Therefore, the arch-adventurer saw that at all hazards this new Procurator must not be allowed to remain in office, for already he had announced his intention to clear the Pravoslavny Church of its malign influences and filthy practices.

Three days later Rasputin went out to Tsarskoe-Selo, where the Emperor happened to be, and entering His Majesty's private cabinet said in a confidential tone:

"Listen, Friend. I have a secret to whisper to thee! Last night I was with Sturmer, and he revealed that a great revolutionary plot is afoot for thy deposition from the Throne!"

"What!" cried the Emperor, pale with alarm as he sprang from his chair. "Another plot! By whom?"

"Its chief mover is the man Samarin, whom thou hast appointed Procurator of the Holy Synod," replied the crafty adventurer. "Sturmer urged me to come at once and to tell thee in private."

"Are you quite certain of this, Holy Father?" asked the Emperor, looking straight into his bearded face.

The monk's grey steely eyes, those hypnotic eyes which few women could resist, met the Tsar's unwaveringly.

"Thou knowest me!" was the "Saint's" grave reply. "When I speak to thee, I speak but only the truth."

That same day Samarin was removed from office and disgraced. Everyone wondered why his appointment had been of such brief duration, but that same night, the Prime Minister Sturmer and Rasputin drank champagne and rejoiced together at the house in the Gorokhovaya, while Anna Vyrubova, the favourite lady-in-waiting, was also with them, laughing at their great triumph.

Not a person in all the great Empire could withstand Rasputin's influence. Honest men feared him just as honest women regarded him with awe. From dozens, nay hundreds, of place-hunters and favour-seekers he took bribes on every hand, but woe betide those who fell beneath the blackguard's displeasure. It meant death to them. He was certainly the most powerful and fearless secret agent of all that the Huns possessed, scattered as they were in every corner of the globe. Yet it must not be supposed that there were none who did not suspect him. Indeed, a certain committee of revolutionaries, to whose action Russia is to be indebted, were watching the fellow's career very closely, and some of the secret reports concerning him here as I write form intensely interesting reading, astounding even for the unfathomable land of Russia.

Within a few weeks of his triumph over the newly-appointed Procurator of the Holy Synod he discovered, with the innate shrewdness of the Russian mujik, that certain secret reports seriously compromising him had been given into the Emperor's hand. His Majesty, in turn, had shown them to his wife. Once again, he saw himself in peril, so, before any action could be taken, he abruptly entered the Empress's room at Tsarskoe-Selo, and boldly said:

"Heaven hath revealed to me in a vision that the enemies of the dynasty have spoken ill of me, have maligned me, and have questioned my divine power. I have therefore come to bid farewell of thee!"

The Empress, who was seated with Madame Vyrubova, and the old Countess Ignatieff, rose from her chair, pale to the lips.

"You—you—you are surely not going, Holy Father!" she gasped. "You cannot mean that you will desert us!" she cried. "What of poor little Alexis?" and the words faded from her lips.

"Yes, truly I am going! Our enemies have, alas, triumphed! Evil triumphs over good in this terrible war," was his slow, impressive answer.

"Of Alexis,"—and he shook his shock head mournfully.

"Ah, no!" shrieked the unhappy Empress hysterically.

"Listen!" commanded the deep-voiced Saint very gravely. "I must not conceal the truth from thee. On the twentieth day of my departure, thy son Alexis will be taken ill—and alas! the poor lad will not recover!"

Madame Vyrubova pretended to be horrified at this terrible prophecy, while the Empress shrieked and fainted. Whereupon the Saint crossed himself piously and, turning, with bent head left the room.

Within half-an-hour he was on his way to his twelve "spiritual brides" in his sordid house at Pokrovsky.

The Empress lived for the next twenty days in a state of terrible dread. Alas! true to the Holy Father's prophecy the boy, on the twentieth day, was seized with a sudden mysterious illness which puzzled the Court physicians who were hastily summoned from Petrograd. Indeed, a dozen of the best medical men in the capital held a consultation, but opinions differed regarding the cause of the haemorrhage, and the Empress again sent wild telegrams urging her pet Saint to return.

Little did she dream that her favourite lady-in-waiting had six hours before administered a dose of a certain secret Chinese drug to the young Tsarevitch and purposely caused the illness which the rascal had predicted.

Time after time did Her Majesty telegraph, urging her "Holy Father" to return and save the boy's life, signing herself affectionately "your sister Alec." Yet the wires were dumb in reply. An Imperial courier brought back no response. The doctors, as before, could make nothing out of the poor boy's illness, and were unable to diagnose it. The charlatan was playing with the life of the Heir of the Romanoffs.

It has, however, been since revealed by analysis that the compound sold to Rasputin by the chemist—a secret administrator of drugs to Petrograd society named Badmayeff—was a poisonous powder produced from the new horns of stags, mixed with the root of "jen-shen." In the early spring when the stags shed their horns there appear small knobs where the new horns will grow. It is from these that the Chinese obtain the powder which, when mixed with "jen-shen," produces a very strong medicine highly prized in China and Thibet as being supposed to rejuvenate old persons, and to act as a kind of love-philtre. When used in strong doses it produces peculiar symptoms, and also induces dangerous haemorrhage.

It is evident from evidence I have recently obtained, that on the twentieth day after Rasputin's departure the high priestess of his cult,

Madame Vyrubova, administered to the poor helpless little lad a strong dose in his food.

Day followed day; she increased that dose, until the poor little boy's condition became most precarious, and the deluded Empress was equally frantic with grief. At any moment he might die, the doctors declared.

One night Rasputin returned quite unexpectedly without having replied even once to the Tsaritza's frantic appeals.

He made a dramatic appearance in her private boudoir, dressed in sandals and his monk's habit, as though he had just returned from a pilgrimage.

"I have come to thee, O Lady, to try and save thy son!" he announced earnestly in that deep raucous voice of his, crossing himself piously as was his constant habit.

The distracted Empress flew to the boy's room where the mock-saint laid his hands upon the lad's clammy brow and then falling upon his knees prayed loudly in his strange jumble of scraps of holy writ interspersed with profanity, that curious jargon which always impressed his "sister-disciples."

"Thy son will recover," declared the saint, thus for the second time impressing upon Her Majesty that his absence from Court would inevitably cause the boy's death.

"But why, Holy Father, did you leave us?" demanded the Empress when they were alone together ten minutes afterwards.

"Because thou wert prone to believe ill of me," was his stern reply. "I will not remain here with those who are not my friends."

"Ah! Forgive me!" cried the hysterical woman, falling upon her knees and wildly kissing his dirty hand. "Remain—remain here always with us! I will never again think ill of thee, O Holy Father! All that is said is by your enemies—who are also mine."

The pious rascal's house in the Gorokhovaya, besides being the meeting-place of the society women who, believers in "table turning," were his sister-disciples, was also the active centre of German intrigues. It was the centre of Germany's frantic effort to absorb the Russian Empire.

Twice each week meetings were held of that weird cult of "Believers" of whom the most sinister whisperings were heard from the Neva to the Black Sea. The "sister-disciples" were discussed everywhere.

The "Holy Father" still retained his two luxurious suites of rooms, one in the Winter Palace, and the other in Tsarskoe-Selo, but he seldom occupied them at night, for he was usually at his own house receiving in secret one or other of his "friends" of both sexes. His influence over both Nicholas II and his German wife was daily increasing, while he held Petrograd society practically in the hollow of his hand. Now and then, in order to justify his title of "Saint" he would, with the connivance of a mujik of his Siberian village, who was his confederate, perform a "miracle" upon some miserable poor person who could easily be bribed and afterwards packed off to some distant part of the Empire so that he, or she, could tell no further tales. A hundred roubles goes far in Russia. The Prime Minister Sturmer, the blackmailer Protopopoff, the dissolute Bishop Teofan, a Court official named Sabouroff, and Ivanitski, a high official in the Ministry for Foreign Affairs, all knew the absurd farce of these mock-miracles, yet it was to the interest of them that Rasputin should still hold grip over the weak-minded Empress and that crowd of foolish women of the Court who had become his "sister-disciples." Oh! that we in Britain were in ignorance of all this! Surely it is utterly deplorable.

The men mentioned, together with half-a-dozen others with high-sounding titles, were bent upon ruining Russia, and giving her over body and soul as prey to Germany. All had been arranged, even to the price they were each to receive for the betrayal of their country. This was told to the Empress time after time by Count Kokovtsov, the Adjunct-Minister of the Interior Dzhunkovsky, the Grand Dukes Nicholas Michailovitch, Dmitri Pavlovitch, and others. But Her Majesty would listen to nothing against her pet "Saint," the Divine director, that disgracefully erotic humbug who pretended that he could heal or destroy the little Tsarevitch. When any stories were told of him, Anna, her favourite lady-in-waiting, would declare that they were pure inventions of those jealous of "dear Gregory's" position and influence.

While Boris Sturmer, frantically scheming for a separate peace with Germany, was with his traitorous gang engineering all sorts of disasters, outrages and military failures in order to prevent the Russian advance, Kurloff, another treacherous bureaucrat, sat in the Ministry of the Interior collecting the gangs of the "Black Hundred," those hired assassins whom he clothed in police-uniforms and had instructed in machine-gun practice.

Rasputin and Protopopoff were now the most dominant figures in the sinister preparations to effect Russia's downfall. Rasputin was busy taking bribes on every hand for placing his associates into official positions and blackmailing society women who, having been his "disciples," had, from one cause or another, left his charmed circle.

Protopopoff, who once posed as our friend and hobnobbed; with Mr. Lloyd George, was a man of subtle intrigue. From being a friend of Britain, as he pretended to be when he came here as Vice-President of the Duma, he was enticed away by Germany to become the catspaw of the Kaiser, and was hand in glove with the holy rascal, with his miracle-working, behind the throne.

Rasputin, himself receiving heavy payments from Germany, had acquired already the most complete confidence of the Tsar and Tsaritza; indeed, to such an extent that no affair of State was even decided by the weak-kneed autocrat without the horse-stealer's evil counsel. Loyal to his Potsdam paymaster, Rasputin gave his advice with that low and clever cunning which ever distinguished him. He gave it as a loyal Russian, but always with the ulterior motive of extending the tentacles of German influence eastward.

In the voluminous confidential report here before me as I write, the disclosures of the rise and fall of Rasputin, I find an interesting memorandum concerning a certain Paul Rodzevitch, son of a member of the Council of the Empire. Alexander Makaroff, one of the three private secretaries of the Emperor, had died suddenly of heart disease, the result of a drinking bout at the Old Donon, and at the dinner-table of the Imperial family at Tsarskoe-Selo the matter was being discussed, Rasputin being present. He was unkempt, unwashed—with untrimmed beard, and a filthy black coat greasy at the collar, and his high boots worn down at heel, as became a "holy man."

The Tsar was deploring the death of this fellow Makaroff, a person whose evil life was notorious in Petrograd, and whose young wife—then only twenty—had followed the example of the Empress, and had become a "sister-disciple."

"Friend!" exclaimed the "Saint" with pious upward glance, for he had the audacity to address the Emperor thus familiarly, "Friend! Thou needst not seek far for another secretary; I know of one who is accomplished, loyal and of noble birth. He is Paul Rodzevitch. I will bring him to thee to-morrow as thy new secretary—and he will serve thee well."

His Majesty expressed satisfaction, for the holy man, the holiest man in all holy Russia, as was his reputation, had spoken.

Next day the good-looking young fellow was appointed, and into his hand was given His Majesty's private cipher. None knew, until it was revealed by the band of Russian patriots united to unmask the spy, that this fellow Rodzevitch had spent two years in Germany before the war, or that he was in receipt of a gratuity of twenty-five thousand marks annually from the spy bureau in the Koniggratzer-strasse in Berlin!

By this means Rasputin placed a spy of Germany upon all the Tsar's most confidential correspondence.

Madame Vyrubova, and the infernal witchdoctor, were already all-dominant. Sturmer and Protopopoff were but pawns in the subtle and desperate game which Germany was playing in Russia. The food scarcity engineered by Kurloff; the military scandals engineered by a certain creature of the Kaiser's called Nicolski; the successful plot which resulted in the destruction of a great munition works with terrible loss of life near Petrograd; the chaos of all transport; the constant wrecking of trains, and the breakdown of the strategic line from the Arctic coast across the Lapland marshes, were all combining to hurl the Empire to the abyss of destruction.

One day the Grand Duke Nicholas visited Tsarskoe-Selo, where he had a private interview with the Emperor—Rasputin's creature, the new secretary Rodzevitch, being present. The Emperor had every belief in the man's loyalty. His Majesty, weak and easily misled, never dreamed of treachery within his private cabinet.

The words spoken by the Grand Duke that afternoon were terse, and to the point.

"The Empire is doomed!" he said. "This verminous fellow Rasputin—the man contemptuously known in the slums of the capital as 'Grichka,' is working out Germany's plans. I have watched and discovered that he is the associate of pro-Germans, and that his is the hand which in secret is directing all these disasters which follow so quickly upon each other."

"But he is a friend of Protopopoff!" the Emperor exclaimed. "Protopopoff has been to England. He has gone over the munition factories in Scotland that are working for us; he has visited the British fleet, and when I gave him audience a few weeks ago, he expressed himself as a firm supporter of our Allies. Read his speech in the Duma only the night before last!"

"I have already read it," replied the Grand Duke. "But it does not alter my opinion in the least. He is hand-in-glove with the monk and with the Duke of Mecklenburg-Strelitz. Why you continue to have either of them about you I cannot imagine. If you do not dismiss them, then the House of Romanoff must fall, I tell you that," he declared quite bluntly.

His Majesty pandered for a moment and replied—"Then I will give orders to the Censor that the names of neither are in future to be mentioned publicly."

This is all the notice the Emperor took of the Grand Duke's first warning. The people did not dare in future to mention "Grichka," for fear of instant arrest.

Since the outbreak of war Mother Grundy has expired in every country in Europe. An unfortunate wave of moral irresponsibility seems to have swept the world, and nowhere has it been more apparent than in Russia.

This unwashed rascal who posed as a saint, who, by his clever manoeuvres, his secret drugs and his bribes, had become so popular with the people, was entirely unsuspected by the simple folks who comprise the bulk of Russia's millions. To them he was a "holy man" whom the great Tsar admired and fed at his table. No one suspected the miracle-worker to be the secret ambassador of the Assassin of Potsdam. Everywhere he went—Moscow, Kazan, Odessa, Nijni, and other cities, he was fierce in his hatred of the Kaiser, and while cleverly scheming for the downfall of his own people, he was yet at the same time urging them to prosecute the war.

A man of abnormal intellect, he was a criminal lunatic of that types which the world sees once every century; a man whose physical powers were amazing, and who though dirty and verminous, with long hair unbrushed and beard untrimmed for a year at a time, could exercise a weird and uncanny fascination which few women, even the most refined, could resist.

The terms upon which Rasputin was with the Empress it has been given to me to reveal in this volume. They would have been beyond credence if the German spy who had been placed as secretary to the Emperor, had been loyal to his unscrupulous employers. But he was not. Money does much in these war-days, and in consequence of a big payment made to him by Rasputin's enemies, the patriots of Russia—and they were many— he intercepted a letter sent by the Empress to her "Holy Father" early in 1916—a copy of which I have in the formidable dossier of confidential documents from which I am culling these curious details.

The "Holy Father" in hair-shirt and sandals had gone forth upon a pilgrimage, and the female portion of Petrograd society were in consequence desolate. The house in the Gorokhovaya stood with its closed wooden shutters. Sturmer was at the Empress's side, but Protopopoff—Satan in a silk hat as he has been called—had gone upon a mission to Paris.

The letter before me was addressed in her Majesty's hand to Rasputin, at the Verkhotursky Monastery at Perm, whither he had retired in order to found a provincial branch of his "Believers" and initiate them into the mysteries of his new religion.

This amazing letter which plainly shows the terms upon which the Empress of Russia was with the convicted criminal from Pokrovsky, contains many errors in Russian, for the German wife of the Tsar has never learnt to write Russian correctly, and reads as follows—

"Holy Father! Why have you not written? Why this long dead silence when my poor heart is hourly yearning for news of you, and for your words of comfort?

"I am, alas! weak, but I love you, for you are all in all to me. Oh! if I could but hold your dear hand and lay my head upon your shoulder! Ah! can I ever forget that feeling of perfect peace and blank forgetfulness that I experience when you are near me? Now that you have gone, life is only one grey sea of despair. There was a Court last night, but I did not attend. Instead, Anna (Madame Vyrubova) and I read your sweet letters together, and we kissed your picture.

"As I have so often told you, dear Father, I want to be a good daughter of Christ. But oh! it is so very difficult. Help me, dear Father. Pray for me. Pray always for Alexis (the Tsarevitch). Come back to us at once. Nikki (the Tsar) says we cannot endure life without you, for there are so many pitfalls before us. For myself, I am longing for your return—longing—always longing!

"Without our weekly meetings all is gloom.

"Only the everlasting toll of war! Germany is winning—as she will surely win. But we must all of us maintain a brave face towards our Russian public. In you alone I have faith. May God bring you back to us very soon. Alexis is asking for you daily. We are due to go to Yalta, but shall not move before we meet here. I embrace you, and so do Nikki and Anna.

"Your devoted daughter, Alec." Has history ever before recorded such an astounding letter written by a reigning Empress to a sham saint?

It must not be thought that Rasputin was without enemies. He had hosts of them, but in an almost incredible manner he seemed to scent danger wherever it lurked, and eluded the various traps set for him. This was probably because he had surrounded himself by creatures ready to do any evil work he ordered. Not only had he earned the most bitter vengeance of wronged husbands and fathers, but he had against him a small league of patriotic Russians, men and women, headed by a civil servant named Vilieff, who had banded themselves together with a view to tear away the veil and unmask the traitor. The rascal knew this, and was ever upon his guard, while Sturmer and Kurloff used their great influence for his protection. At the same time Rasputin had corrupted the Russian Church in its centres of power and administration until nearly half its high ecclesiastics were agents of Germany.

In order to exhibit a swift, relentless hand in dealing with any enemy who should arise against him, Rasputin one evening cordially invited Vilieff, who had sworn to open the eyes of the people to the mock-monk's villainy. Indeed, he had travelled to far-off Pokrovsky and collected much damning evidence concerning Grichka's past. Kurloff was at dinner to meet the young man, the bait offered by Rasputin being that the official of the Ministry of the Interior intended to promote him to a highly lucrative post in his department.

According to a statement made by the monk's wily accomplice, Yepantchine, who afterwards came forward and made so many revelations, only the trio sat down to dinner, whereupon the traitorous bureaucrat openly suggested that the band he had formed against Rasputin should be betrayed to the Palace police, in return for which he had ready for him five thousand roubles in cash, and, in addition, would there and then appoint him to a lucrative position in the chancellerie of the Ministry.

On hearing this, the young man sprang up and angrily denounced both monk and minister as traitors, declaring that he would at once expose the effort to purchase his silence.

Without further ado Rasputin drew a revolver and, secretly approaching him, shot him dead.

His body was found in the snow near the corner of the Kazanskaya early next morning. The dead man's friends, who knew of his visit to Rasputin that night, informed the police, but the monk was already before them.

At dawn he sought the Emperor at the Tsarskoe-Selo, and found him in his dressing-gown. To him he complained that enemies were making a disgraceful charge against him, and added:—

"I seek thy protecting hand, friend. Wilt thou give orders to the police to leave me unmolested?"

The Emperor, who believed in him as implicitly as his wife, at once gave orders over the telephone, and thus the murder was suppressed.

A week later a man named Rouchine, who had, with Yepantchine, assisted him in his mock-miracles, discovered him with a certain Swede named Wemstedt, who was chief of the German Secret Service in Stockholm, and who had come in disguise to Petrograd to obtain certain reports furnished by Sturmer. His secret visit to Rasputin's house was to get the documents for transmission to Germany, and to make one of the large monthly payments to the monk for his services as the Kaiser's agent.

Their meeting was watched by Rouchine, who overheard greater part of the conversation of the pair ere the "Saint" became aware there was an eavesdropper. Instantly he scented danger, for he trusted nobody; the monk made no sign, but when Wemstedt had gone he placed a bottle of vodka in a spot where he knew that Rouchine would find it.

As he expected, his servant drank a glass, and within half-an-hour he expired in terrible agony, with Rasputin jeering at him in his death-throes.

It is computed that during 1916 no fewer than twenty persons lost their lives in consequence of visits to that sinister house within the shadow of the Winter Palace. Armed with those secret Chinese drugs, the pious assassin could administer baneful doses which proved fatal hours afterwards, with symptoms which completely deceived the doctors.

Knowing his own danger, he one day hit upon a new plan for his own protection, and when at dinner at the Imperial table he, addressing the Empress, said:

"A vision of the fixture hath to-day been revealed unto me! It is a warning—one that thou surely shouldst heed! When I die, Alexis will live but forty days longer. Surrounded as I am by those who seek my downfall and death, I know not what plots may be formed against me. I only know that assuredly Alexis will only survive me through forty days. If God wills it, my end may be to-morrow!" he added, raising his eyes piously.

At this the Empress betrayed terrible distress. But the ruse of the wily scoundrel worked well, for the personal protection at once afforded him by order of the Tsar was as complete as the surveillance upon the Emperor himself.

IV

The "Hidden Hand" of Berlin

Rasputin, though revealing himself constantly as a blasphemous blackguard, had by the middle of 1916 become the greatest power in Russia. Through his good offices Germany hoped to crush the Empire.

Examination of the confidential reports concerning his scandalous activities here before me causes me to halt aghast that the Imperial Court, which I attended in peace time, Petrograd society, and the hard-working classes in Russia, should have become so completely and so utterly hypnotised by his disgraceful "religion." The latter had eaten into the Empire's heart, causing an outburst of open and disgraceful immorality in the higher circles—a new "sensation" that was appalling. In Moscow, Kazan, Tambov, and other cities, "circles" of the "Sister-Disciples" had been eagerly formed, together with a branch which were meeting in secret at a small old-world monastery called Jedelevo, in the Province of Simbirsk, and about whose doings many scandalous whispers reached Petrograd.

"Grichka" possessed the reputation of being a popular preacher. That was not so. He had never been ordained a priest; he was a pure adventurer, and did not belong to any ecclesiastical order. Therefore he had no licence to preach in a church. He was simply a Siberian peasant convicted of theft, blackmail, and outrage, who had set himself up to be a "holy man." And as such, all Russia, from the Empress downwards, accepted him and swallowed any lie that he might utter. Truly the whole situation was amazing in this twentieth century.

He preached often to his "sister-disciples" in their *salons*, and sometimes at "At Homes," where fast society women who had fallen beneath the pious scoundrel's fascination hoped to make other converts. To such "At Homes" only young and pretty women were ever invited. Rasputin had no use for the old and angular.

One evening one of these reunions for recruiting purposes was held by the yellow-toothed old Baroness Guerbel, at her big house in the Potemkinskaya, and to it a young married woman, wife of an officer named Yatchevski, who was well-known in Petrograd, had been invited. Her husband, hearing of this, called three of his own burly Cossacks, and next night they concealed themselves close to Rasputin's house. There they waited until the bearded "holy man" emerged to go upon his usual evening visit to the Winter Palace; when the men suddenly sprang upon him, and hustling him into a narrow side street, stripped him of his finely embroidered silk shirt, of the usual Russian model, his wide velvet knickerbockers, and his patent-leather top-boots. After that they administered to the fellow a sound and well-deserved thrashing, having first gagged and bound him. Afterwards they placed him, attired only in his underwear, upon a manure heap in a neighbouring stable-yard, while the clothes they had taken from him were packed in a big cardboard costume-box and delivered by special messenger privately to the Empress at the Palace.

Her Majesty was, of course, furiously indignant that her dear "Father" should thus be made sport of. At once a rigid inquiry was ordered, but the perpetrators of the well-merited punishment were never discovered.

Rasputin was ever active as head of the camarilla. The attention of the Holy Synod had time after time been called to the amazing exploits of this pious charlatan, until at last it was deemed expedient to hold yet another inquiry, into the fellow's conduct.

Supplied with German money, he employed spies on every hand to keep him informed of any untoward circumstances, or any undue inquisitiveness. So he quickly heard of this proposed inquiry and consulted Bishop Teofan, brother of one of his favourite "sister-disciples," who lived in Siberia. That night both Monk and Bishop sought the Tsar and Tsaritza. Rasputin declared angrily that there was a most formidable plot against himself. He therefore intended to leave Petrograd, and return to Siberia for ever.

"Because by divine grace I possess the power off healing, thy Church is jealous of me," he declared to the Emperor. "The Holy Synod is seeking my overthrow! Always have I acted for the benefit of mankind, and so through me thy dear son is under God's grace. But the Russian Church seeks to drive me forth. Therefore, I must bow to the inevitable—and I Will depart?"

"No! No!" cried the Empress in despair. Then, turning quickly to her husband, who had left some important business of State, which he was transacting in his private cabinet with the War Minister, Her Majesty exclaimed:

"Nikki. This ecclesiastical interference cannot be tolerated. It is abominable! We cannot lose our dear Father! Order a list of his enemies in the Church to be made, and at once dismiss them all. Put our friends into their places."

"If thou wilt leave matters entirely to me," said the sham saint, addressing the feeble yet honest autocrat, "I will furnish the list, together with names of their successors."

"I give thee a free hand, dear Gregory," was the Emperor's reply. Within twelve hours all those in the Russian Church who had sought to unmask the pious rascal found themselves dismissed, while in their places were appointed certain of the most drunken and dissolute characters that in all the ages have ever disgraced the Christian religion, their head being the arch-plotter Bishop Teofan.

About this time, after many secret meetings of the camarilla at Rasputin's house, Protopopoff succeeded in bribing certain generals at the front with cash—money supplied from Germany, to prevent a further offensive. In consequence, at a dozen points along the Russian lines the troops were defeated and hurled back. This created exactly the impression desired by the camarilla, namely, to show to the Russian people that Germany was invincible, and that a separate peace was far preferable to continued hostility. It was to secure this that Rasputin and his gang were incessantly working.

Scandal after scandal was brought to light, and more than one officer of the high Russian command was arrested and tried by court-martial. Rasputin and Protopopoff had now become more than ever unscrupulous. Generals and others who had accepted bribes to further Germany's cause were secretly betrayed to the Ministry of War, care, however, always being taken that they could produce no absolute evidence against those who had previously been their paymasters.

A notorious case was that of General Maslovsky, who, before the war, commanded the Thirteenth Army Corps at Smolensk. He, with General Rosen, commandant of the Twenty-third Army Corps at Warsaw, had been induced by a "sister-disciple" of Rasputin's—a pretty young Frenchwoman—to accept a large sum paid into his account at the Volga Kama Bank in Moscow, provided that the Russians retreated in the Novo Georgievsk region. This they did, allowing great quantities of machine-guns, ammunition and motor lorries to fall into the enemy's hands.

In order to create scandal and public distrust, the "holy man" secretly denounced these two traitors, who were arrested and tried by court-martial at Samara. The prisoners in turn revealed the fact that big payments had been made by the young Frenchwoman. So she, in turn, was also arrested. Rasputin, however, did not lift a finger to save his catspaw. She declared that she had simply been the tool of the mock-monk, but the latter privately informed the President of the Court that the young Frenchwoman was a well-known spy of Germany known to the Court, and whom he had held in suspicion for a considerable time.

No word against Rasputin's loyalty was ever believed, for was he not the most intimate and loyal friend of both Emperor and Empress? Therefore the court-martial found the prisoners guilty, and the trio paid the penalty of all spies—they were shot in the barrack-square of Samara!

This is but one illustration of Rasputin's crafty intrigue and cool unscrupulousness. Possessed of a deeply criminal instinct as he was, it was impossible for him to do an honest action. He never failed to betray his friends, or even send them to their graves upon false charges secretly laid, if by so doing he could further his own despicable ends.

The dissolute rascal, possessed of superhuman cunning, held Russia in the hollow of his hand, and aided by his fellow-scoundrel, Protopopoff, he could make or break the most powerful men in a single hour.

That he was in active communication with Germany, and that the vile plots against the Russian arms were being manufactured in Berlin, is plainly shown by the following letter, which after his death was discovered, together with a quantity of other highly incriminating correspondence—which I shall disclose later—in a small safe concealed beneath the stone floor of the well-stocked wine-cellar at the house in the Gorokhovaya.

It is in one of the sentence-ciphers of the German Secret Service, but fortunately in the same safe the de-cipher was found, and by it that communication as well as others is now revealed.

The letter is written upon thin pale-yellow paper, so that it might be the more easily concealed. It had probably been bound up in the cardboard cover of a book and thus transmitted. This letter before me reads as follows:—

Number 70
August 16th, 1916
"Your reports upon the activity of Krusenstern (Commander of the 28th Army Corps), and also upon the friendship of

Sakharoff and Yepantchine (two prominent members of the Duma), is duly noted. The firm of Berchmann Brothers, of Kiev, are paying into the Credit Lyonnais in Petrograd 120,000 roubles to your account, with a similar sum to your friend S. (Boris Sturmer, Prime Minister of Russia).

"Instructions are as follows: Suggest to S. this plan against the Duma. From the archives of the Ministry of the Interior he can obtain a list of the names and places of residence of thousands of Russian Revolutionists of the extreme school. These he can, if we order it, place in prison or have them tried by court-martial and shot. He will, however, act most generously and secretly. He will, under promise of protection send them forth as his agents, well supplied with funds, and thus arrange for a considerable number of pro-German Social Democrats to enter Petrograd and work alongside the Russian Anarchists, Tolstoyans, Pacifists, Communists and Red Socialists. With such a widespread propaganda of wild and fierce agitators in the munition factories, we shall be able to create strikes and commit outrages at any moment instructions are given. They should be ordered to continually urge the working men to strike and to riot, and thus begin the movement that is to make Europe a federation of Socialist republics. This plan attracts the working-class, and has already succeeded on the Clyde and in Ireland. Your only serious opponent is Gutchkoff, but you will arrange with the Empress that his activities be at once diverted into another sphere.

"Enlist on our side as many members of the Duma as possible. Furnish from time to time a list of payments made by you, and the firm of Berchmann will sustain your balance at the Credit Lyonnais.

"We await the result of your good services, which are highly appreciated by His Majesty, and which will be amply and most generously rewarded when we have Russia in our hands, which will not be long.

"Messages: Tell S. (Sturmer, the pro-German Prime Minister and a creature of the Empress) to be extremely careful of the Grand Duke Dmitri. He holds a compromising letter written by Nada Litvinoff regarding her attempt to suborn Brusiloff. The woman Litvinoff is reported to be staying at the Regina Hotel in Petrograd. No effort should be spared to obtain and destroy that letter, as it is very compromising. Professor Miliukoff should be removed. Ten thousand roubles will be paid for that service. J. or B. might be approached. Both are in need of money.

"Instruct Anna (Madame Vyrubova) to tell the Empress to receive a woman named Geismann, who will demand audience at noon on August 30th. She carries a verbal message from the Emperor. It is important that you should know Countess Zia Kloieff, of Voroneje. She possesses influence in a certain military quarter that will eventually be most useful and highly essential.

"H—(a spy whose identity is up to the present unknown) has fixed August 29th, at 11:30 A.M., for the disaster at the shell-filling factory at Krestovsky. An electric line is laid beneath the Neva, and all is prepared.

"Salutations from all three of us.

N.

Such were the secret instructions received from Berlin by the murderous charlatan who posed as one of the most loyal Russians in the Empire.

His reply, of which a copy is appended—for strangely—enough he was a businesslike rascal—is as follows. It is brief but to the point:—

"Yours and remittances received. S. already at work. Have informed Her Majesty. All is being prepared for our great coup. The more disasters and loss of life in munition factories the better the impression towards yourselves. S. has already sent four hundred extreme revolutionists to the front with money and instructions. Have noted all your points. Martos takes this to Helsingfors, and will await your reply with any further orders.

"Have had no instructions concerning the Englishman C. Please send. Suggest imprisonment upon false charge of espionage. If so, please send incriminating papers to produce as evidence.

G.

The scoundrel's reply here before me is, in itself, in his own handwriting, the most damning evidence against him.

That Sturmer and Protopopoff acted upon those instructions has since become apparent. Events have shown it. Puppets in the hands of the Emperor William, with money flowing to them in an ever-endless stream from businesslike sources entirely unsuspected by the highly patriotic banks handling those substantial amounts, they were swiftly yet surely undermining the greatness of the Russian Empire and seriously cutting the claws of the Russian bear. The "Russian steam-roller," as certain English prophets—oh! save them!—were so fond of calling the Muscovite army in the early days of the war, was growing rusty for want of proper lubrication. Rasputin and his friends were placing its machinery in the reverse gear by their marvellously well-concealed intrigues, and their lavish distribution of money to those long-haired revolutionists who had honestly believed that by removing the autocrat they would liberate their dear Russia.

No plot more subtle, more widespread, or more utterly amazing has ever been conceived in the whole world's history than the one which I am here disclosing.

A convicted criminal, a mere unmannered and uncouth peasant from far Siberia, held both Emperor and Empress of Russia beneath his thumb. He gave to both of them orders which they weakly obeyed. If one of the erotic scoundrel's "sister-disciples" asked a favour—the appointment of lover or of husband to a lucrative post—he went at once to the Emperor, and actually with his own illiterate hand wrote out the orders for His Majesty to sign.

And to that unkempt blackguard, who seldom indulged in the luxury of a bath. Her Majesty the Empress bowed her knee, honestly believing that the Almighty had endowed him with powers superhuman, and that he could cause disaster or death whenever he willed it.

Further amazing and incriminating letters are before me as I write, and I shall print more of this secret correspondence in order that readers in Great Britain may know the depths of Germany's villainy and the exact methods by which Russia has been betrayed.

The official *dossier* concerning the crimes and conspiracies of the arch-scoundrel is astounding. It becomes increasingly amazing as one turns over its voluminous pages, its confidential reports, its copies of telegrams dispatched under fictitious names, since obtained from the telegraph bureaux of Russia, and its originals of secret instructions from Berlin.

In the latter one finds the subtle hand of the notorious Steinhauer, the head of the Kaiser's spy-bureau, the fair-bearded, middle-aged

Prussian who accompanied the German Emperor to Buckingham Palace on his last visit to London, and who was one of the select party of German motorists who came to tour England with Prince Henry of Prussia at their head.

It devolved upon myself to accompany and watch that tour very closely. Even then one department in Whitehall had not been chloroformed by the dope of the Sleep-quietly-in-your-beds Party—a department in the formation of which I had had some hand. Steinhauer I had met in Germany, though he did not know me, and when he came to England with His Imperial Highness, as Herr Eschenburg of Stuttgart, driving his big red "Mercedes," I considered that it was high time to keep a strict eye upon him—which I did. What I discovered of his movements and of his associates has been of greatest advantage since the outbreak of war.

No more expert spy exists in all the world today than "Herr Eschenburg of Stuttgart", whose real name is Steinhauer, known in the German Secret Service as "Number Seventy."

The *dossier* here placed at my disposal shows that Herr Steinhauer visited Rasputin in Petrograd four times before August, 1914, while his underlings arrived at the house in the Gorokhovaya many times after the two Empires had come to grips.

Rasputin, in his unique position as autocrat aver the Autocrat, felt himself the personal agent of the Kaiser, and as such seems to have somewhat resented Steinhauer's rather arrogant orders. Indeed, he complained bitterly to the German Emperor, who, in reply, propitiated the Siberian peasant by explaining that he was so occupied by the campaign against his enemies that he left all matters of detail to "our trusted and loyal friend Steinhauer, whose actions and orders are as my own."

On August 28th, 1916, there arrived in Petrograd a pretty dark-haired young Dutch woman named Helene Geismann. She presented a letter of introduction to Rasputin that evening at his house, and was promised audience of Her Majesty the Empress at noon next day.

The monk was at Tsarskoe-Selo when the young woman called. It was a meeting day of the higher, or Court Circle of the "sister-disciples," such seances being held at five o'clock each Friday afternoon.

Three new "disciples" had been initiated into the mysteries of the mock-pious rascal's new "religion." Their names were the Baroness Zouieff, and Mesdemoiselles Olga Romanenkoff and Nadjezda Tavascherne, the two latter being of the noblest families of Moscow, and all moving in the Court entourage.

Nicholas II was away at the front, therefore Rasputin on such occasions ruled the Empire, and actually signed with his own hand orders and appointments, as His Majesty's representative. When the Emperor was absent the dirty, unkempt peasant, who called himself a monk, usurped his place in the Imperial household.

Through this unprincipled scoundrel and blackmailer Germany was cleverly working to undermine and effect the fall of the Muscovite Empire. No expense was being spared, nor were there any scruples. Germany intended that the Russian defensive should crumble.

When the Empress received the young woman Geismann, an emissary from Berlin and the bearer of several documents, including an autograph letter from the Kaiser, the "Holy Father" was also present. The superstitious, neurotic Empress could do nothing without the advice of the man who had by his mock-piety and his sensuous "religion" so completely entranced her. She, like her weak, narrow-minded husband, had become completely hypnotised by the dissolute charlatan, in whose hands lay absolute power.

When the Kaiser's messenger presented the secret letter to the Empress, she also handed another to Rasputin.

This was found among the contents of the safe in the basement of "Grichka's" house, and is in German, as follows:—

"*Strictly private and confidential.*
> General Headquarters in France, Montmedy,
> August 10th, 1916

"Your excellent service to our Empire has been reported to me by Herr Steinhauer. I congratulate you, happy in the knowledge that the Empress Alexandra has, in yourself, such a good and wise counsellor. You have done much, but there is still more good work for you to accomplish.

"Your friends must see that there is an increasing lack of material and ammunition, that information reaches Berlin regarding orders for guns, explosives and automobiles placed in England, in order that we can watch for them near the Finland coast, and destroy them. Disasters on railways, in munition works and elsewhere are advisable. Steinhauer is sending you six trusted agents to effect these. Your friends must afford them official protection, and they must be also afforded opportunity.

"I have also sent certain suggestions to Her Majesty the Empress which she will discuss with you. Your two most dangerous enemies at the moment appear to be Prince Yuri Lvov, who has a great following, and the man from Tiflis, M. Cheidze. If their activities could be ended, you would be in far less danger. It may be possible for you to arrange this. Consult with the Empress. It is my Imperial will that the payment arranged between us shall be doubled from this date. Salutations.

Wilhelm R. and I.

Could any letter be more incriminating? The Kaiser, with his constant appeals to Almighty God, was suggesting outrage and assassination to his paid agent—the man who, aided by the Prime Minister Sturmer and the blackmailer Protopopoff, held the future of Russia in his unwashed hands!

For half-an-hour the young Dutch woman, the Kaiser's secret messenger, was kept waiting in an ante-room while the Empress consulted with her "Holy Father." Then at last Her Majesty handed the woman an autograph letter to take back to the Emperor William. All that is knows of the contents of that note is that it contained a promise that Germany should triumph.

What chance had poor suffering Russia against such crafty underhand conspiracy? Every one of her proposed military movements were being betrayed to Germany long before they were executed, and thousands of lives of her fine soldiers were daily being sacrificed, while the arch-traitor Rasputin continued his career of good-living, heavy-drinking, and bi-weekly "reunions."

At these meetings the blackguard usually crossed his hands upon his breast, and with appalling blasphemy declared himself sent by the Almighty to deliver Russia from the invader.

Towards all—to society, to those of the immoral cult that he had founded, to Russia's millions, he posed as a stern patriot. Every one believed him to be so. If not, surely, he would not be so closely intimate with their Majesties they argued. Nobody in Russia dreamed that he was the agent of the Kaiser, or that the Empress had full knowledge of the great plot in progress.

In the following month there occurred a number of mysterious disasters. Four explosions occurred in rapid succession; two at Petrograd, one at Moscow, and one at Kostrovna, all involving considerable loss of life, while troop trains were derailed at several important junctions, and other outrages committed, by which it was apparent that German agents were actively work. Yet the police were powerless to detect the perpetrators of these dastardly acts. Truly the black eagle of Prussia had struck its talons deep into Russia's heart.

Late one night Rasputin was carousing at his house with the Prime Minister Sturmer and two "sister-disciples," young married women whose names were Baroness Gliuski and Madame Pantuhine, well-known in Petrograd society for their loose living, and who were helping the plotters and receiving large sums from German sources for their assistance. The "Father" had only an hour before returned from Tsarskoe-Selo, where he had knelt at the bedside of the poor little Tsarevitch and then performed a pretended miracle. The truth was that Madame Vyrubova had administered to the boy in secret several doses of that secret drug with which the mock-monk had provided her. In consequence, he had become ill and his Imperial mother had once again called Rasputin to "heal" him. This the fellow did, for Madame Vyrubova withheld the dose, and within four hours of Rasputin placing his dirty hands upon the poor boy's brow and uttering those cabalistic nine words of jargon from one of the blasphemous prayers which the scoundrel had written for use by the "sister-disciples," the heir had recovered. And in that way, with his degenerate confederate, the rascal worked his "miracles."

The four were seated around the monk's dining-table, smoking and drinking, the two women ever and anon devotedly kissing the "saint's" dirty hands, when his body-servant entered with a note for his master. As Rasputin read it his face fell.

"Danger!" he gasped.

"What is it?" inquired the bearded Prime Minister eagerly, putting down his glass of champagne untouched.

"Letchitzki! He is arrested!"

"Letchitzki!" echoed Boris Sturmer, who was in uniform, as he had been to a diplomatic function at the United States Embassy that night. "This is indeed serious for us! Why is he arrested? Who has dared to do that?"

"Goutchkoff, Minister of Munitions, has ordered his arrest for embezzlement—ninety thousand roubles!"

"Curse Goutchkoff!" cried Sturmer, starting up. "In that case, our friend Protopopoff, as Minister of the Interior, is powerless to act in his interest!"

"Is it really very serious?" asked the fair-haired young Baroness, who was at that moment holding the "saint's" hand.

"Serious!" cried the uncouth Siberian peasant, who had so completely hypnotised both the women. "Very. If his trial took place he would certainly expose us! We cannot afford that. He has sent me this secret message placing the onus of his release upon me, and I must secure it at once. He has documents, letters I have written him. If they were found, then the whole affair must become public property!"

"That must not be!" declared Sturmer. "At any moment Miliukoff, or that young lawyer Kerensky, may get to know."

"Kerensky was again arrested yesterday at my orders for his speech in the Duma," said Rasputin. "I agree. The prosecution of Letchitzki must not proceed. It is far too dangerous."

"Is there anything I can do?" asked the pretty Baroness, one of the most unscrupulous women in Russia.

"Yes," replied the monk. "You know the Minister Goutchkoff. Go to him early to-morrow morning, and appeal on Letchitzki's behalf. Take with you ninety thousand roubles which I will give you as soon as the banks open. Pretend to the Minister that he is your lover, that he has embezzled the money to pay for presents to yourself—then hand over the sum missing."

"Excellent idea!" declared Sturmer. "You are always ingenious when cornered, Gregory!"

"By that we shall clear the way for further action. We must both see the Empress at once. It is not yet too late," Rasputin added, and the merry quartette at once broke up, the "sister-disciples" to their own homes, and the monk to drive to the Palace.

Both conspirators, so well-known, passed the sentries unchallenged, and traversing the long corridors to the private apartments, went by the gigantic Cossack on duty at the end, and through the big swing-doors to the luxurious wing of the great Palace.

It was already long past midnight, and the only person they could find was the Tsar's eldest daughter, the Grand Duchess Olga, who had with the eldest of her sisters entered Rasputin's "sisterhood" a year before. Every one, including the servants, had retired. The Princess, who was reading an English novel in her own little sitting-room, appeared surprised to see the "Holy Father" at that hour, but took from him an urgent message to the Empress.

Ten minutes later the Tsaritza, in a dainty lace boudoir-cap and rich silk kimono, entered the room where the pair of scoundrels awaited her.

When alone, Rasputin revealed the fact of Letchitzki's arrest, adding:

"Thou canst realise the great danger to us all. If that man is brought before the Court believing that we have not endeavoured to save him, he will, no doubt, reveal and produce certain letters I have sent to him. Our plans will then become public, and Russia will rise and crush us! At present they do not suspect thee of any pro-German leanings. Thou art the great and patriotic Tsaritza. But if this prosecution proceeds, then assuredly will the truth become known!"

"But, Holy Father, what can I do?" asked the weak hysterical woman, alarmed and distracted.

"Thou must telegraph at once to thy husband to order the prosecution to be dropped," said the crafty scoundrel, standing in that erect attitude he was so fond of assuming, with one hand upon his breast and the other behind his back.

"I will do all that you wish," was her eager response, and she sat down at once to write the message to the Tsar who, on that night, was with his gallant soldiers at the front.

> "Paul Letchitzki, Under-Secretary of the Ministry of
> Munitions, has been arrested for embezzlement of public
> funds," she wrote. "It is highly necessary, for our peace,
> that the prosecution shall be instantly stopped. Every
> moment's delay means danger. I will explain when you return.
> Telegraph your order for his immediate release and the end of
> all proceedings against him. I await your acknowledgment.
>
> Alec

Then, having read the telegram, of which both men approved, she gave Rasputin her golden bangle from her wrist. From it was suspended the tiny master-key of the escritoire in her boudoir.

"Will you, my Holy Father, fetch me my private cipher-book?" she asked the mock-monk, at the same time bending and kissing his hand.

The fellow knew where the little book was kept in such privacy, and in a few moments he had brought it. Then Sturmer at once sat down and put the message into cipher, afterwards taking it himself to the clerk in the telegraph room on the other side of the Palace, for transmission to the Emperor.

At ten o'clock next morning a reply in code was handed to the Empress. When, with the aid of her little book, she de-coded it, she read:

"I cannot understand how the prosecution of a thief of whose name I am ignorant can affect us adversely. I have, however, at your desire ordered his release and the suppression of all proceedings.

Nikki

To this, the Tsaritza, after she had sent a copy of the reassuring despatch to Rasputin, replied:

"I thank you for your kind generosity. How noble of you! Accused was an innocent victim of his enemies, and our action shows that you are open and just. Our Father and myself anxiously await your return.—Alec." The moment Rasputin received the message from the hands of the trusted Cossack, Ivan Khanoff, the personal guardian of the young Tsarevitch, whom the Empress trusted with all her private correspondence, he telegraphed to Boris Sturmer at the Ministry of Foreign Affairs, telling him of the order of the Tsar.

And both laughed triumphantly at each other over the telephone. Yet both certainly had had a very narrow escape of exposure, and for the first time the Tsaritza saw the handwriting on the wall.

V

Rasputin's Secret Orders from Berlin

Some pages of Rasputin's *dossier* concern his intimate friendship with the Imperial family, and more especially with the Tsar's daughters, whom the Empress herself had placed beneath his "tuition" and influence.

It seems that the monk Helidor—who because of his patriotism fell out of favour when Rasputin commenced to perform his conjuring tricks, which the Imperial Court believed to be miracles—still retained his friendship with the Grand Duchess Olga, and the governess of the Imperial children, the honest and straightforward Madame Tutcheva.

To Helidor—who afterwards revealed all he knew to the Revolutionary Party—the young Grand Duchess confessed her love for a certain very handsome officer, Nicholas Loutkievitch, of the Imperial Guard. She saw him often in the vicinity of the Palace, and also when she went to church, and he used to smile at her.

"Holy Father," she said one clay to Helidor, "what can I do? I love him. But alas! love is forbidden to me—for I am an Imperial princess. It is my torment."

Helidor had tried to console her by saying that she was young, and that she would love many times before she found the man who was to be her husband. It was surely not strange that the handsome young Grand Duchess should be attracted by a handsome man, for after all, even Imperial princesses are human.

Helidor, who belonged to the Pravoslavny Church, under Bishop Teofan, saw Rasputin a few days later and incidentally mentioned the youthful infatuation of the young Princess.

"Oh! I have already cured all that!" said the scoundrel with a laugh. "Her infatuation has been dispelled. I have cast the devil out of her." Then Rasputin boastingly disclosed to Helidor certain things which left no doubt in the latter's mind as to the true state of affairs existing at Tsarskoe-Selo, or the truth of what Madame Tutcheff had alleged.

Indeed, among the filed pages of the *dossier* which deal with this particular incident, is a letter which I venture here to reproduce. Rasputin, with all his mujik's shrewdness, preserved many letters written to him by women of all grades, hoping that when cast out of the Imperial circle he could use them for purposes of blackmail. Here is one of them:

Palace of Peterhof
March 23rd, 1916

Holy Father,

Dear true friend, we are all desolate without you. When are you returning from Pokrovsky? You promised to be here on the third, yet we have had no word from you. Dear true friend and father, how is Matroysha (Rasputin's peasant wife)—and the children? Give my love to them. Tatiana and I are sending them some things by the courier to-day. Each time we go to Anna's (Madame Vyrubova) all is but blank despair. We miss our sweet and helpful reunions, and long always for your return. You, my holy Father, are my inestimable friend. I no longer think of Nicholas, but of you alone, and of our holy religion. My mother is desolate without you. Pray for me. I kiss your dear hands.

Your loving daughter,
Olga

I copy this from the great mass of papers before me—the documentary evidence of the tragic story of the downfall of the great Imperial House of Romanoff—in order that the reader may be able to form some slight idea of the marvellous, almost incredible grip which Germany had upon the Tsar's family, his household and his nation through the medium of the verminous peasant who had declared himself a Heaven-sent apostle of God.

The moral atmosphere of the Court was shocking. Rasputin, chief agent of the Kaiser, was posing, just as the Kaiser himself posed, as a God-fearing, prayerful man sent by Divine-right as a deliverer. The monk's mission was, however, to deliver Russia into the hands of Germany.

The next pages of the *dossier* contain advice notes of German funds paid to the "saint" through the most unsuspicious channels.

As instance of these I copy the following dates and extracts, the actual letters of advice themselves being of a pretended business character and of no importance:

April 6th.—Payment to His Excellency Boris Sturmer by Jules Wick, Morskaya 57, advocate, sum due from the estates of the late Baroness Nikeleuko, of Doubno.—78,600 roubles.

April 18th.—Payment made to Gregory Rasputin by Nicholas Pokotilo. Address Select Hotel, Ligovskaya 44, Petrograd, representatives of Messrs. Solovoioff, of Odessa.—62,460 roubles.

June 1st.—Payment to His Excellency D.A. Protopopoff made for rent of lands at Vyazma, by Alexander Koltchak, agent of the estate of Prince Tchekmareff, less 15 per cent, commission to Messrs. Montero and Company, of Kieff;—21,229 roubles.

June 3rd.—Payment to Vera Zoueff, dancer at Luna Park, by G. Merteus, Nevsky 81, Petrograd.—13,000 roubles. (The woman who passed as a Russian was one, Bertha Riehl, a German dancer, and a secret agent of Berlin.)

June 17th.—Payment to Sophie Tatistcheff (who had married Baron Roukhloff, one of the Tsar's secretaries who had control of his Majesty's private correspondence), by Safonov's Bank, in settlement of an insurance claim for property destroyed by fire at Poltava.

I have copied these in their order of sequence, but the items number over one hundred, and reveal payments of huge sums of German secret service money to Rasputin and his friends, thus forming a most illuminating disclosure as to the manner in which Russia was rapidly being undermined.

With such dark forces at work in the very heart of the Empire, it is indeed marvellous that General Brusiloff could have effected his superhuman offensive between Pripet and the Roumanian frontier. He started with his four armies early in June, 1916, and by the middle of August had captured 7,757 officers, 350,845 men and 405 guns. Berlin became seriously alarmed at such a situation. All Rasputin's plotting with Sturmer, Count Fredericks, Protopopoff, Countess Ignatieff, Madame Vyrubova, and a dozen other less prominent but equally importunate officials, together with all the steady stream of German marks flowing into Petrograd could not stem the Russian tide on the

German and Austrian front's. The Russian "steam-roller" seemed really progressing.

The Kaiser grew seriously alarmed. At the instigation of Count von Wedel, his right-hand in espionage and unscrupulous propaganda, a secret message was sent to Rasputin—a message which he preserved among his other papers. It runs as follows, and is in the German cipher of the Koniggratzer-strasse of which the mock-monk kept a de-cipher in his interesting safe. Hence it has been available:

"F.G. 2,734–22.
"Memorandum from 'Number 70,' August 29th, 1916.

"It is deemed of extreme urgency that the offensive of the Pripet should at once cease; and be turned into a victory for the Central Powers as promised us in your despatch of July 1st. You are not keeping faith with us! What is wrong? S. (Sturmer, the Prime Minister) is inciting the Russians to victory in his speeches.

"His triumphant telegrams to Asquith must cease. They only serve to encourage the Allies. This advance must not continue. Further, the munition factories at Vologda and Bologoye have not yet been destroyed as we ordered. We know that K. (a clock-maker named Kartzoff who blew up the explosive works at Viborg in which 400 lives were lost), who did such good work in that direction, is arrested and shot, together with the woman R. (Mdlle. Raevesky, whose father was in the Ministry of the Interior under Protopopoff). We note that you gave information to the police concerning both persons, because they became lovers and were likely to open their mouths and thus become dangerous to us.

"*Secret Instructions:*—That to Nicholas Meder be entrusted the task of destroying the Vologda and Bologoye works, and that Madame Fleischer, who lives in Volkovo, be appointed as his assistant—each to receive six thousand roubles for their services.

"As your efforts to prevent the offensive in the Pripet region have failed up to the present, it is ordered that General Brusiloff be removed by the means already employed in other enemy countries. Send a trustworthy messenger to Doctor Klouieff, living in the Vozkresenskaya, in Kazan, to ask for 'a tube.' He will know. The contents of the tube introduced into any drink will produce tetanus—with a rapid end. Klouieff is German, and may be entirely trusted. Brusiloff has a body-servant named Ivan, Sawvitch who is a friend of Boris Koltchak, a soldier in the 117th Infantry Regiment of Muisk. Koltchak, who has been in our service for five years, is to be ordered and facilities rendered him to visit his friend Sawvitch at General Headquarters, and to introduce the contents of the tube into Brusiloff's food or drink. For this service you are ordered to pay in secret twenty-five thousand roubles upon its completion. The man Sawvitch is in love with the sister of Koltchak, a fact which will ease certain difficulties. Be careful, however, of Marya Ustryaloff, who is jealous of the woman in question.

"General Korniloff may be removed by the accidental explosion of a hand-grenade, in the same manner in which General Zhukovsky was removed in March last at Pultusk. This service could be entrusted to the soldier Paul Krizhitsky, of the 17th Grenadiers of Moscow, who is a despatch-rider and constantly at the General Headquarters. He should examine the bomb—a pine-apple one, in preference, and release the pin by accident. For this service you can pay in secret up to eighteen thousand roubles.

"Further, it is urgent that you should induce the Emperor at once to order the release of the men Polenov and Levitsky, and the woman Erich, who were arrested in the Hotel Brosi at Vitebsk. Their papers, if found, must be restored to them. The documents are probably stored in the strong rooms of either the Ootchotny Bank, in the Hevsky, or at Lampe's. So get hold of them, as they contain facts incriminating S. (Sturmer) and V (Madame Vyrubova). It is of most urgent importance that the prosecution in question be dismissed, and further, that those who instigated it should be degraded in pursuance of our policy. For this service you will be granted a generous extra payment. S.—70." The signature, scribbled in blue ink upon these remarkable instructions, is that of the notorious Herr Steinhauer, the Kaiser's chief spy and controller of the whole secret ramifications of Imperial Germany throughout the civilised world. I venture to publish it in these pages in order to show the devilish cunning of Germany, and their frantic efforts, by any underground and dastardly means, to stem the tide of war which threatened to overwhelm them.

In consequence of these instructions Rasputin immediately set to work to execute the wicked command of His Imperial Master in Berlin.

On the day following that secret message being delivered into his hands by a woman dressed as a peasant, as, descending from his carriage, he entered a house in the Nevski, he walked into the Emperor's private study and, placing his hand across his breast in that mock-pious attitude he so often assumed, he said:

"Friend! Thou hast always been held by thy people to be a just and honest ruler; but in Vitebsk those who act in thy Imperial name are acting illegally and persecuting two poor men and a woman with motives of revenge. God has placed His holy protecting hand upon our dear Russia, and has given victory unto our gallant Brusiloff. But if injustice be done in thy Imperial name then the Divine Providence will most assuredly withdraw protection from us."

"What is this, Holy Father?" asked the Emperor in great surprise.

"At Vitebsk two men, Polenov and Levitsky, together with a woman called Erich, three patriotic Russians who have, been engaged in Red Cross work—have, because of the ill-will of the Governor Wauthier, been apprehended, and false charges instituted against them."

"Of what nature?"

"Of communicating with the enemy—a vague charge which to-day may be made against even the most patriotic," replied the monk, the "Holy Father" of the Empress, standing in that same attitude he had at first assumed. "From the Holy Father of the monastery at Vitebsk I have received a confidential, and urgent report that the Governor Wauthier, an ill-living official, has instituted these false charges in order to conceal his own disgraceful misdeeds, which the woman Erich has threatened to expose."

Then, after a pause, the dissolute monk and secret agent of the German Emperor said in that insolent, familiar manner he assumed when addressing the Tsar:

"Friend! This Governor, against whom the Holy Father at Vitebsk sends me secret information, should be dismissed and disgraced, and thy three innocent subjects released. If thou wilt permit injustice in thy Empire, then the success of thy arms cannot be maintained."

"Holy Father," said the weak impotent monarch, "the Governor shall be dismissed. Pass me over a telegraph-form."

And Rasputin took from the writing-table one of the forms upon which the Tsar wrote his autocratic orders, and actually at the monk's dictation His Majesty wrote an order for this release of the prisoners and the dismissal of the innocent, patriotic Governor, against whom the lying agent of the Kaiser had, according to his instructions from Berlin, laid a charge!

Truly the great patriotic Russian Empire had already fallen beneath the "Mailed Fist," even though thousands of her sons were daily sacrificing their lives to secure her freedom.

On the day following, Petkoff; who had already opened his separatist propaganda among the Ukrainian prisoners, in favour of Germany, arrived hot-foot in Petrograd, and spent some hours with Rasputin at his house, where the Prime Minister Sturmer and His Excellency Protopopoff were also closeted. The secret meeting was held at three o'clock and lasted until eight, when one of the Imperial carriages came from the Winter Palace, as it did daily, to convey the "Holy Father" there.

The Emperor had left again for the front three hours before, but the Empress remained. The dirty monk at once sought her, explaining that Germany had reached the last limits of her power upon the eastern front, and urgently needed a slackening of the Russian offensive.

"It is truly God's will that our friends the Germans shall not be crushed!" declared the cunning blackguard. "Are we not told that if we are smitten by an enemy upon one cheek we should turn the other? I declare to thee that if we press our enemies further, then the wrath of God will assuredly fall upon thy house—and upon thy son the Tsarevitch," he said in his low base voice, crossing himself piously the while.

Indeed, that night, so deeply did the charlatan impress the poor Empress that she sat trembling at the fate which must be Russia's should Brusiloff's victory be maintained.

Incredible as it may seem, the Kaiser now held Russia in the hollow of his hand. No despatch from Petrograd to the Allies; no order for material; no communication of whatever sort, Imperial, diplomatic or private, but copies were at once transmitted to the Wilhelmstrasse, where the negotiations were known as soon as they were in Downing Street—and sometimes sooner!

Within a fortnight of Rasputin's grim prophecy of Russia's downfall if she further defied the Imperial power of Germany, the cunning plot to infect General Brusiloff with tetanus was attempted by the soldier Koltchak, while in a train conveying him from Borisoff to Petrograd, on a flying visit to consult with the Minister of War. Happily the plot failed, but the coffee in which the deadly culture had been placed was, alas! unfortunately drunk by a certain Major Dobrovolski, who died mysteriously and in great agony four days later; the General, of course, being entirely ignorant of Berlin's vile plot against him.

An attempt was also made upon General Korniloff at Chernitsa ten days later. A soldier who had no business near, handled a hand-grenade carelessly, just as the General happened to be riding by. The bomb exploded, killing the General's horse on the spot, but he himself escaped with a deep cut over the left eye. Everybody, of course, believed it to be a pure accident, therefore the affair was never reported.

These two attempts upon the lives of Russia's military leaders, the documentary evidence of which exists, were only the forerunners of several others even more ingenious and more desperate, as I shall later on disclose in these pages.

The failure of the attempts to assassinate Brusiloff and Korniloff, and the continuation of the Russian offensive, now caused the greatest consternation in Berlin, where it was believed that Rasputin was neglecting the work for which he was being paid so heavily.

A message was conveyed to him through Swedish sources telling him of the Kaiser's extreme displeasure at the failure of the plans, and reminding him of His Majesty's words when he had had secret audience and accepted the Imperial proposals to become chief agent of Germany in Russia. Certain further instructions were also given as matters of extreme urgency. The Russian progress had aroused the most serious fears in Berlin.

Meanwhile the monk's ambition knew no bounds. With marvellous cunning he was busy blackmailing a number of unfortunate society women who, having entered his cult, had afterwards abandoned it, and while being the practical ruler of Russia, because of the Tsaritza's devotion to him, yet he was daily plotting with his pro-German friends for the nation's downfall.

At each of the reunions of his sister-disciples he would strut about and play the part of "saint." On each occasion he would declare: "If you repulse me, God will abandon you! I am the chosen of God—sent to deliver Holy Russia!"

To those who were sceptical he would speak more plainly and convincingly, saying "If you do not obey me, then I will see that you are punished by my friends." So by this means he surrounded himself by an increasing number of hysterical women whose wealth he exploited, and from whom he took bribes to procure high places, distinctions and decorations for their husbands and brothers or their lovers.

Indeed, before him the highest officials in the Empire bowed, crossed themselves, and kissed his hand—not because he was a priest— but because they constantly feared lest they should incur his displeasure, well knowing that if they did, they would at once be superseded.

At Peterhof, or at Tsarskoe-Selo, the actions of the bearded blackguard were believed to be inspired by Providence. This dissolute Siberian fakir, the Madame Vyrubova, and her Imperial mistress, the

Tsaritza, formed a trinity which ruled the Empire at war; and thousands of brave Russian soldiers died in consequence.

The pro-German propaganda, fostered in secret by the dissolute three, was permeating every department of the State, and was even being spread among the armies at the front. At each success of the Russians the Empress would grow irritable and despondent, while the slightest success of the enemy caused her to be wildly jubilant. One day, at one of the seances of the higher circle of Sister-Disciples held at Tsarskoe-Selo, news was conveyed to Her Majesty that the Germans were retreating and that their fortified base at Vladimir Volgnsk, near Lutsk, had been captured. Thereupon the Empress cried in great distress:

"Why is this allowed! Why is this advance against the Germans not stopped? Russia will never crush Germany. She shall not do so! Holy Father! pray for our dear Germany!"

"O Sister! In thy heart harbour neither fear nor distrust, for indeed God hath revealed unto me that there will be a separate peace and the ultimate triumph of the German arms," replied the mock-saint, assuming his most pious attitude, with his hands crossed upon the Russian blouse of rich dark blue silk deeply embroidered with gold, which it was his habit to wear at the seances at Court. "While on my pilgrimage last week with Father Macaire, in the Monastery of Verkhotursky, I had a vision."

"A vision!" echoed the Empress, while her daughter Olga and a dozen ladies of the Court sat agape and eager. "Holy Father, tell us of what has been revealed," urged Her Majesty.

"I saw hosts of men entering a great city as conquerors—hordes from the west bringing to us all the benefits and a higher civilisation. I saw His Majesty the German Emperor advance and grasp the hand of thy Imperial husband the Tsar, and kiss him fraternally upon both cheeks. And over all was set the halo of God's glory, and Russia rejoiced that she had cast off the yoke of her Allies."

"God be thanked!" gasped the Empress hysterically. "Then we need no longer fear. Truly Heaven is good to send thee to us, dear Father!" she added, taking his rough hand, with its bulgy knuckles and unclean nails, and kissing it fervently, while all her Court echoed the words so constantly used at the gatherings of the cult: "Holy Father! God be thanked that we are thy chosen sisters."

On the following day, however, Rasputin having returned to his house in Petrograd, a secret meeting was held at the house of a man named Roukhloff, situate in the Vereiskaya. The meeting was convened by certain of the monk's enemies in order to expose him as an impostor and a charlatan. It must be remembered that none dreamed that the scoundrel was the direct secret agent of the Kaiser himself, or that Sturmer and Protopopoff were anything else than fine sterling Russian patriots. All three were urging every one to "get on with the war."

And with this in mind it induces one to wonder whether a similar farce is not to-day being played in certain political circles in other countries of the Allies!

Rasputin had many friends, but he had also made many bitter enemies. As an outcome of that secret meeting, the man Roukhloff, son of a functionary in the Ministry of Foreign Affairs, defied the authorities and publicly denounced the "Saint" as "a dangerous erotic humbug." The effect was electrical. The Emperor, with the Empress, Count Fredericks, and Madame Vyrubova, was in the Imperial train, travelling to the Crimea. The moment of that hostile attack was well-chosen, and for a time the "Saint's" position was a precarious one. But as soon as it became known in Petrograd that he had been denounced, his house was crowded by his faithful sister-disciples, who would have no word said against him.

He at once announced his intention to return to Siberia, and addressing them with his usual mock piety, said:

"The people of Petrograd have cast out the man sent to them by God. I will return to my monastery at Pokrovsky, and pray for their salvation. Assuredly God will punish the disbelievers. You, my sisters, keep faith in your belief. If I never return—then pray for me."

An hour afterwards the impostor left for the Nicolas Station, accompanied by a crowd of women-believers of all classes, but instead of travelling to Siberia he changed his route at Moscow and hurried in the track of their Majesties. Meanwhile, the ill-living Archbishop Teofan, who had declared that he "heard in the Holy Father Rasputin the voice of God," and that to hound him from Petrograd meant the incurring of the Divine displeasure and the downfall of the Empire, and Bishop Hermogene, another of the monk's creations who had also belauded him, now both saw an opportunity of denouncing the monk's duplicity and malpractices, and thereby securing the favour of the people for themselves.

This they did, and in consequence a great sensation was caused in society, both in Petrograd and in Moscow. In the Duma, Rasputin was openly denounced by M. Goutchkoff, a man of large experience and who had worked in the Manchuria campaign and done much to assist the Grand Duke Nicholas and General Alexeieff in the munition crisis of 1915. He was Director of the Committee of War Industries, and had, introduced into this committee some highly capable Labour delegates, who were now no longer blinded by the halo of sanctity which Rasputin had assumed for himself.

Thus a storm suddenly burst over the head of the holy rascal who had practised his abominations under his pseudo-religious cloak, and who was at the same time secretly plotting for the triumph of Germany.

But so cleverly did he juggle with the future of the Russian Empire that he went post-haste across Europe, down to Yalta in the Crimea, and on arrival drove through the pine woods to the Imperial Palace. He arrived there at six o'clock in the morning, after a long and fatiguing journey. But such was his iron nerve and strong constitution that he was as fresh as when he bade farewell to his clinging devotees in Petrograd who had so fervently kissed his dirty hands.

He had the audacity to go straight to the Tsar's dressing-room, and there met His Majesty as he was coming from his bath. Naturally Nicholas II was surprised, and on inquiring the reason of his unexpected visit, the "Saint" exclaimed:

"They have driven me, the man of the Lord, from Petrograd! I go back to Siberia to dwell there in peace. But God will now assuredly weak vengeance upon Russia, and all that she holds most dear—as well as upon thy son and heir."

"But, Holy Father!" gasped the Emperor, "what has happened? Tell me."

As the Tsar sat in his red bath-wrap, the unwashed "Saint" made explanation that both the Church and the Duma had declared him to be an impostor, adding:

"I will not trouble myself over those who defame me. They are as dust. God has sent me to Russia, and the Russians have despised me."

"But who are your enemies?" asked His Majesty anxiously.

That was the question which Rasputin intended that the Emperor should ask. At once he explained that the Archbishop Teofan and Bishop Hermogene had both turned against him, and in consequence the Tsar called his servant to bring him a telegraph-form at once.

"Whither shall I send those persons?" asked His Majesty.

"Nowhere. Let them work their evil will against thy Empire. God will himself punish them!" replied the fakir and ex-thief who had self-assumed the title of "Father."

"I shall leave to-night for Siberia, and shall not return."

"No. Forgive them, Holy Father," urged the Emperor apprehensively. "For my sake and for Russia's sake forgive them. I will send Teofan, your false friend, to the Taurida, and Hermogene shall retire to the monastery of Tobolsk. Helidor, too, is no friend of yours. He shall be sent to prison."

"Thy will shall be done regarding the two first, but spare Helidor. He may yet be useful unto thee," was the crafty mujik's reply.

"Is there any other enemy who should be removed?" inquired the Emperor. "Tell me, Holy Father—and I will deal with him if you will still remain with us. If you leave, poor little Alexis will die."

The mock-saint, sprawling his legs in the Emperor's dressing-room, reflected for a few moments. He knew that by his own hand Russia was ruled.

"Yes," he said presently. "God has told me to forgive my enemies. I will do so if thou wilt assist me. Too little consideration is given to our friends."

"All consideration shall be given them. To whom do you refer?"

The monk drew from beneath his, long black habit a scrap of paper already prepared, and consulting, it, said:

"I wrote down here yesterday certain appointments which should be given to those who support thee, against thy enemies." It was a list of favours which the rascal had promised to women for their male acquaintances, and from each he would receive a generous *douceur*, according to the means of the person indicated.

"You will note Ivan Scheveleff, of the Imperial chancellerie. He has served thee well for the past five years, and should have the title of Excellency, and consequent promotion," said the religious rascal. "Again, there is Sergius Timacheff, of the Imperial printing works, who should be appointed a privy councillor; and Madame Grigoiovitch, who is in the Peter-and-Paul prison, should be released and amends made to her for the false charge upon which she was convicted at the instance of Michael Alexandrovitch."

"I will telegraph orders in each case," was the Emperor's reply, as he lit a cigarette prior to his valet entering.

"And the salary of the Minister Protopopoff is far too little. It should be increased by at least one-half. He is thy most devout and devoted friend and servant of Russia."

"That shall be done," was the monarch's weak reply. Little did His Majesty dream that Protopopoff was one of Russians traitors.

"Brusiloff should be watched, as there is evidence of treachery against him. Before the war he was friendly with a man named von Weber, an agent of Germany. Nekrasov, Minister of Communications, is also a traitor, and should be dismissed," said the monk, thus denouncing two of Russia's strongest and most patriotic fighters, who were perfectly innocent.

"It shall be done," replied the Emperor quietly. "Father, I am glad you have, told me." Indeed, owing, to the false statements of pro-German police officials, General Brusiloff was within an ace of arrest a week later. The Minister Nekrasov, however, received his dismissal, Protopopoff being one of his enemies, and in that manner was the monk playing Germany's game.

Thus the evil power of this arch-scoundrel was paramount. By his influence men were made and broken daily. Indeed, to-day dozens of men who because of their suspicion of the saint's "divinity," incurred the blasphemer's displeasure are, languishing in gaol in various remote parts of the Empire, while German agents occupied some of the "highest offices in Russia," while the head of the Church of holy Russia had been appointed by the unwashed blackguard himself.

As proof of this interview at Livadia, the *dossier* of Gregory Rasputin, the Siberian Cagliostro, which is before me, contains the following letter:

Rizhsky Prospect, 37

My dear Father,

I have heard that you have left upon a pilgrimage to your own monastery in Siberia. May God be with you, and bless you. To-day my title of Excellency is officially announced. My bankers have passed to yours the sum of 30,000 roubles. There will be a further sum of 10,000 roubles passed if you will kindly send me, under cover, those two letters of the Countess Birileff. I await your reply.

Ivan Scheveleff

Rasputin's mania for filing his correspondence is the basis of our true knowledge of his astounding career and activity, for the next folio in the *dossier* is a copy of a blackmailing letter he wrote a few weeks after his visit to the Crimea, to the man Sergius Timacheff. It reads as follows:

Friend,

It is now many days since His Majesty appointed you Privy Councillor of the Empire, but I have received no word from you or from your bank as we arranged. If I receive nothing by next Thursday, the facts concerning your son's implication in the Platanoff affair (the blowing up of a Russian battleship in the Baltic by German agents) will be passed on to the Admiralty. If double the sum we arranged passes to my bank before the date I have named, I shall remain silent. If not, I shall take immediate action.

G.

The "holy" blackmailer was becoming more and more unscrupulous. Behind him he had the Emperor and Empress, soothed to sleep by his marvellous cunning and his mock miracles. Incredible as it seems, he was able to evade all the many pitfalls set for him by his enemies, because he swept them all from his path by Imperial orders and stood forth alone as the "Holy Father," sent by Providence to create a new and prosperous Russia.

He had no fear of death. He wore a shirt of mail, and the Palace police, the same ever-alert surveillance as that placed upon the person of the Tsar himself, kept a watchful eye upon him, though through Protopopoff they had orders to relinquish their watchfulness at any moment the "Saint" deemed it necessary.

He frequently deemed it necessary if he held his conferences with Sturmer, Protopopoff, Anna Vyrubova, and the small camarilla of persons who were being so richly rewarded by mysterious incomes from estates they did not possess—or, plainly speaking, by money from Berlin.

Rasputin saw that in order to keep faith with his "sister-disciples" in Petrograd, it was necessary for him to journey again to his Siberian village. He therefore declared to the Emperor that he had much business there, and promised that he would return to Peterhof as soon as the Imperial family arrived there.

When the Tsar of all the Russias had bent and kissed the monk's filthy hands, and promised that his orders should be despatched at once by telegram to Petrograd, the monk sought the Empress, told her what had occurred, explaining how his enemies had denounced "the man sent by God." The Tsaritza sat appalled. Could the Russian people have denounced her "Holy Father"? To her it seemed impossible. She bent before the rascal and wept bitterly.

"Oh, Sister!" he said in his deep voice, "I will retire to Pokrovsky until these enemies of Russia have been discomfited and defeated. Then, verily, I will return to stand beside thee and fight as thy friend, as God has commanded me."

Then he took his leave and travelled to the so-called "monastery" he had established in his far-off Siberian village—the big house in which a dozen of his female devotees were so eagerly awaiting him.

VI

Rasputin's Secret Instructions from Berlin

Now that Rasputin's amazing career is being here investigated, chapter by chapter, the facts disclosed seem almost incredible, but, of course, such a situation could only have occurred in a country where nearly ninety per cent, of the priest-ridden inhabitants are unable to read or write, and which is in most things a full century behind the times.

Surely in no other country in all the world to-day could an illiterate, verminous mujik, who had actually been convicted and punished for the crimes of horse-stealing, falsely obtaining money, and assaulting two young girls, be accepted as a Divine healer, a "holy" man, and the saviour of Russia. Here was a man whose whole life had been one of scandalous ill-living, a low drunken libertine of the very worst and most offensive class, actually ruling the Empire as secret agent, of the Kaiser!

By the clever ruse of establishing his cult of "sister-disciples" he had so secured the ears of the weak-kneed Emperor and his consort, that whatever views he declared to them they at once became law. So amazingly cunning was he that he realised that the only way in which to retain the hold he had established at Court was now and then to absent himself from it, first making certain "prophecies," the fulfilment of which could be effected by his secret friends.

As often as he uttered a prophecy and left Petrograd upon one of his erotic adventures—to found provincial circles of the cult of Believers— so surely would that prophecy come true. He foretold the downfall of one official, the death of another upon a certain date, a further relapse of the Tsarevitch, and so on, until their Majesties held him in awe as heaven-inspired. In the high Court circle of which he was the centre, this "Holy Father" could do no wrong, while his most disgraceful exploits, scandals unprintable, were merely regarded as mundane pleasures allowable to him as a "saint."

No reign since the days of the Caesars was more fraught by disgraceful scandals than those last days of the *regime* of the ill-fated Romanoffs. The

Roman empresses were never traitors as the Tsaritza most certainly was. Can any one have sympathy with the once-Imperial, afterwards exiled to Siberia—that same zone of that illimitable tundra to which the Tsar of all the Russias had exiled so many of his innocent and patriotic subjects, men and women who fought for Russia's right to live, to expand, and to prosper? Let us remember that in Siberia to-day lie the bones of a hundred thousand Russian patriots, persecuted under the evil *regimes* of Alexander and of Nicholas. In the days of the ex-Tsar's father I went to Siberia, and I visited the convict prisons there. I saw convicts in the mines chained to wheelbarrows by forged fetters, and I saw those poor tortured wretches who worked in the dreaded quicksilver mines of Nertchinsk, their teeth falling out and their scalps bare. Of what I myself witnessed, I years ago placed on record in black and white. Those reports of mine will be found in the public libraries of Great Britain. But to-day they do not concern the reader of this book only inasmuch as they furnish proofs, with others, of the oppressive hand of the Romanoffs upon the devoted and long-suffering people of Holy Russia—"Holy"—save the mark! The erotic rascal Rasputin was in himself a striking example of the men who control the Paroslavny Church.

This mock-pious blackguard, to whose artful cunning and clever cupidity has been due the death of hundreds of thousands of brave Russians of all classes in the field, held the fortunes of the great Empire within the hollow of his dirty paw.

The contents of the big *dossier* of his private papers disclose this satanic scoundrel's double-dealing, and the true terms in which he stood with the Wilhelmstrasse.

To me, as I study the documents, it is astounding how accurately the Germans had gauged who were their actual friends in Russia and who were their enemies. Surely their sources of information were more astounding and more complete than even the great Stiebur, the King of Spydom, had ever imagined.

It sterns that while Rasputin was living a dissolute life at the "monastery" he had established in his far-off native village of Pokrovsky, he received many telegrams from Tsarskoe-Selo, both from the Emperor and Empress, urging him to forgive his traducers and to return. To none of these he responded. One day, however, he received a telegraphic message which came over the wires as a Government one, marked "On His Imperial Majesty's Service," from Madame Vyrubova. Its copy is here before me, and reads:

"Return at once to Petrograd. A dear friend from afar, awaits you. It is most urgent that you should come back at once. There is much to be done.

Anna

Such an urgent summons showed him that his presence was required. He knew too well that the "dear friend" was a German agent sent in secret to see him.

Therefore he bade farewell to his dozen "sister-disciples," the head of whom was the opulent "Sister Vera," sister of the dissolute Bishop Teofan whom Rasputin himself had created. Teofan was a fellow-criminal of his who had been imprisoned for horse-stealing in Tobolsk, and now he wore richly embroidered ecclesiastical robes and bent the knee before the altar daily.

In consequence of this message from his friend Anna, Rasputin hastened back to Petrograd.

Now Madame Vyrubova was Rasputin's tool throughout. Hers had been a strange history. Her past had been shrouded in mystery, yet I here disclose it for the first time. As Mademoiselle Taneieff, daughter of the director of the private chancellerie of the Tsar, she became five years before one of the maids-of-honour of the Empress. A pretty, high-spirited girl, she at first amused and afterwards attracted the neurotic spouse of the stolid, weak-minded Autocrat. In due course she married a rather obscure but good-looking naval officer named Vyrubova—a lieutenant on board the cruiser *Kazan*. The husband, after a year at sea, learned certain scandals, and therefore he went one night boldly to the Emperor—who happened to be at Peterhof—and asked that he might divorce his wife.

His Majesty was both surprised and angry. He made inquiry, and discovered a very curious state of affairs—a scandal that had been hushed up and is now revealed by the new light shining upon Russian Court life and the internal scandals of the Empire.

Briefly put. His Majesty found that his wife the Empress had fallen in love with a certain General O—. The dark-haired Madam Vyrubova had acted as go-between for the couple—a fact which her husband knew, and threatened to expose as a vulgar scandal if the Emperor did not allow his divorce! It seemed that General O—had rather slighted the Empress, and had taken up with a certain Princess B—, who had been on the stage, and who was declared to be one of the prettiest women in all Russia. The General had followed the beautiful princess to Cairo. A week later at Assouan, in Upper Egypt, he had been seized by a mysterious illness and died. The explanation given to the Emperor by the husband Vyrubova was that the General had fallen a victim to the jealousy of his wife the Empress.

The Tsar made secret inquiry, and to his surprise found that all the officer had asserted had been correct. Madame Vyrubova had at the Empress's orders followed the General and arranged his death. Therefore His Majesty could do nothing else than allow the officer to divorce his wife, who, truth to tell, was the catspaw of the poisoner Rasputin, who held her in his grip.

These widespread ramifications of the mock-monk's influence and his power created by the judicious expenditure of German palm-oil are utterly astounding. The more deeply one delves into this voluminous *dossier*, the more amazing does it become, until the enemy's wicked attempts to undermine Russia, our ally, almost stagger belief.

When Rasputin at last returned to Petrograd, in response to the orders of the handsome Anna, he was handed a secret communication from Germany.

This confidential despatch, as it lies here before me, speaks for itself. It is in a German letter-cipher, different from all the others, and for a considerable time it defied all efforts, to decipher it. At last it was accomplished by the Russian Secret Police, and it certainly reveals a most dastardly series of amazingly cunning plots. Here it is:

Memorandum 26874.327

"'Number 70' is sending to you Sister Molfetta, of the Italian Red Cross, whose number is 168. She will leave Berlin on the 3rd prox, and travel by way of Gothenburg. Please inform P. (Protopopoff) and request him to give her his protection and prepare her dear passport. She will stay at the house of B. (Bukoff, a furrier in the Vereiskaya, who was a German agent and assistant to Rasputin); you will call upon her there.

"The object of her mission is to cultivate friendly relations with the barrister Alexander Kerensky, who, though at present obscure, will, it is here believed, shortly make his influence felt very strongly against us. The woman 168 has orders to compromise him, and afterwards create a public scandal in order to discredit him in the eyes of the public.

"Further, we seriously view the strength of Kerensky and the influence he may exert in the prosecution of the war, therefore we leave it to your personal discretion whether or not he should be removed. Number 168 possesses the means, and will act upon your orders.

"*Secret Instructions.*—You are to inform His Majesty in confidence that M.I. Tereshchenko (now Minister for Foreign Affairs) is dangerous, and should be arrested. If his house in Kiev is searched, compromising papers which have been placed there by S. (a German agent named Schumacher) will be discovered. Tereshchenko is threatening to expose your friend S. (Sturmer, Prime Minister), and should it once be suppressed by imprisonment.

"The letter herewith enclosed please give into the hands of Her Majesty the Empress in secret. Also inform her that the wishes she has expressed in her last letter to His Majesty shall be carried out.

"You are to inform S. and P. (Sturmer and Protopopoff) that the shortage of food in Russia is, owing to Birileff's indecisive policy, not sufficiently marked. He must be dismissed upon grounds of incompetence, and they must appoint a new Food Controller who will, connive, by holding up supplies, to create a famine. An epidemic, if spread in Moscow, Kazan, Kharkow, Odessa, and other cities at the same time as the famine, would greatly contribute towards Germany's success. The matter has already been discussed, and an outbreak of cholera suggested. You should consider the suggestion at your end, and if you decide upon it, the necessary steps can easily be taken, though we consider nothing should be done in Petrograd, because of yourselves and the Imperial family.

"The bearer of this will remain in Petrograd four days, and then bring back any news you can send regarding the future situation. Matters are now becoming desperate with us. Hindenburg has decided that at all hazards we must withdraw troops from your frontier, and send them to the west. We rely upon you and your friends to create a famine, for which you will receive increased gratuities, as in the case of the retreat from Warsaw."

Thus will it be seen that the "holy" blackguard, the right-hand and adviser of the Emperor Nicholas, was posing as the saviour of the great Russian Empire, whom Great Britain was supplying with munitions of war, and while he was everywhere declaring that Brusiloff's strategy would wreck the German offensive, yet at the same time he was plotting famine and pestilence in the very heart of the Empire!

None knew this secret—except the German-born Tsaritza. From her, Rasputin held back nothing. In secret he showed her all the despatches he received from the Koniggratzer-strasse. His influence upon Her Majesty at this stage is made vividly apparent by significant remarks which he made to Sturmer on the night after his return to Petrograd, and the delivery into his hands of that cipher despatch from Berlin as revealed above.

"My dear Excellency!" he said, tossing off a glass of vodka and eating some caviare at the great carved sideboard in his own room before sitting down to dinner, "you have been speaking of the Tsar and the Tsaritza. To the Tsar I am Christ, the saviour of Russia and the world! Their Majesties salute me; they bow to me and they kiss my hand. What higher sphere can I achieve? The Imperial children prostrate before me; they kiss my hands. Ah! my dear Excellency, I could disclose to you things which—well, which I could not relate without blushing!"

It was at this period, when a friend of the "holy" peasant, Striaptcheff, a fellow-thief of Pokrovsky and a man convicted of burglary, pressed his attentions upon the "Holy Father" and demanded an appointment. Incredible as it may appear, yet the criminal in question was six days later appointed as a bishop of the Russian Church, with the usual fat emoluments, and he could scarcely read or write. Truly Holy Russia was progressing beneath the Rasputin *regime*. She had a burglar as bishop.

Meanwhile, the monk proceeded at once to carry out his secret orders from Berlin.

We know that the camarilla held council a week later, and that Sturmer, Protopopoff, Striaptcheff—who had now become inseparable from Rasputin—as well as Manuiloff, an ex-journalist who conducted the secret police under Sturmer, were present at the monk's house. At the meeting the false Red Cross sister from Berlin was also present.

It was agreed that it would be best to remove Kerensky, who, though a headlong enthusiast, would be a very difficult man for a woman to compromise. It was known that he possessed secret sources of knowledge regarding the intention of the camarilla to betray Russia into Germany's hands, therefore the woman Molfetta was given orders to carry out her plot, to secure his assassination at the hands of a renegade Jew of Warsaw named Levinski, who was ready to commit any crime if paid for it.

The attempt was made three weeks later. While Kerensky, who lived to become afterwards Prime Minister of the new Government, was turning the corner by the Alexandra Hospital to cross the Fontanka to the Sadovaya, late one night, on his way home to the Offitzerskaya, he was shot at three times by the fellow Levinski. Each shot happily went wide, and as a result Alexander Kerensky still lives to pilot Russia to her freedom.

The manner in which the traitorous camarilla brought about a famine in the capital, and in certain districts in the Empire, until the people of Petrograd paraded the city crying "Give us bread, or end the war!" is well known to all. But how they attempted to carry out the dastardly orders of Berlin to create an epidemic of cholera at the same time, I will reveal with quotations from official documents in the next chapter.

VII

The Plot to Spread Epidemics in Russia

In my work of unmasking Rasputin I find that constant secret communications were at that time passing between the "holy" scoundrel and his infamous paymasters in the Koniggratzer-strasse, while messages were continually being exchanged in strictest confidence between the Kaiser and the German-born Tsaritza, who lived beneath the thraldom of this common horse-stealer.

Berlin, with all its devilish inventions for unfair warfare prohibited by the Hague Convention, had not overlooked the fact that owing to the primitive sanitation of Russia, epidemics had very often been widespread and most difficult to stamp out; therefore the suggestion to artificially produce outbreaks of bubonic plague and Asiatic cholera in the heart of the Empire had been suggested to that traitor, the Prime Minister Boris Sturmer, and his fellow-conspirators of the "camarilla," of whom the Siberian charlatan known as "Holy Father" was the head. While the Imperial Court bowed its knees to the erotic rascal, yet strangely enough the people doubted him, and in secret jeered at him. The satanic suggestion from Berlin, however, appealed to the camarilla of pro-German plotters.

The Russian army was gallantly holding out, even though many traitors held highest commands. The Germans had reached the height of their offensive power on that front, and a separate peace with Russia was in Berlin admitted to be, highly necessary, if the ultimate success of their arms was to be achieved. Therefore, if a devastating epidemic broke out, then Sturmer would have excuse to go to the Tsar and strongly urge the necessity for peace as the only salvation of the Empire.

Hence the necessary steps were at once taken by the conspirators who were in the habit of meeting almost daily in the Gorokhovaya. Proof of what was on foot is disclosed by the following secret despatch from Berlin, which is included in Rasputin's private papers, which so fortunately fell into the hands of the patriotic party of Russia. I here reproduce it:

Memorandum 26932.366
"'Number 70' has placed your communication and suggestions before a high quarter, and they are all approved. He is

sending you, by way of Malmo, Karl Johnke, whose number is 229, a bacteriologist of the Frankfort Institute, who will arrive in Petrograd on the 18th, and seek you. By the same ship will arrive, consigned to our friends the firm of Yakowleff and Company, wholesale fruiterers, of the Nikolskaya, in Moscow, one hundred and twenty-six barrels of Canadian apples, with ninety cases of Canary bananas. These will be distributed in the ordinary course of trade to Kazan, Kharkow, Odessa, and other centres. See that P. (Protopopoff) grants easy facilities for rapid transport to the consignees in Moscow, as they are perishable.

"'Number 229' has full instructions to deal with Ivan Yakowleff, who is our 'fixed post' in Moscow, and who is receiving his instructions in secret by the messenger who brings you this. The fruit must not be handled or eaten, as it has been treated and is highly dangerous.

"Cholera should occur within three weeks of the arrival of the fruit. We rely upon P. taking steps to facilitate its rapid delivery. Some of it should be presented to charitable institutes for distribution among the poor.

"Inform A. (Anna Vyrubova) that Korniloff (General Korniloff, whom all know to be one of the most successful of Russian generals) suspects her concerning the Zarudni affair and has at his house some correspondence which is incriminating. It is in a cupboard in his bedroom and should be secured at once. (G. Zarudni was active in political law cases before the Revolution, and has since been appointed Minister of Justice in the Kerensky Cabinet.) Zarudni is working against both S. (Sturmer) and yourself. If an accident happened to him it would render the atmosphere more clear. The same applies to his friend N.V. Nekrasov, who is on the Duma Budget Committee and on the Railway Committee. Both may upset our plans.

"Against General Ostrogradski, Inspector-General of Cavalry, a charge of treason should be made. The bearer brings documents in order to arouse suspicion that he has sold military secrets to Austria. These can be produced at his trial. His continued activity against us, and his hatred of yourself are both dangerous.

"'Number 229' will make personal reports to you concerning the negotiations with Roumania and also regarding the efforts we are making to prevent war material from England reaching Russia.

"'Number 70' notes with gratification that the explosion at the nitro-glycerine works at Viborg has been effected, and that the factory was totally destroyed and most of the workmen killed. Please pay E. (an analytical chemist named Paul Eck, who was a friend of Rasputin's) the sum promised.

"It would be best if their Majesties removed to Tsarskoe-Selo. Anna Vyrubova should cultivate Boris Savenkov, Commissioner to the Seventh Army. (This suggestion shows the remarkable foresight of Berlin, for to-day Boris Savenkov is acting Minister of War.) You yourself should lose no time in becoming acquainted with Countess Vera Kokoskin, who lives at Potemkinskaya, 29. She is eager to meet you. Admit her as a disciple, for being an attractive and ambitious woman, she has considerable knowledge of what is in progress in certain quarters in the Duma. Being in want of money, and being blackmailed by a penniless lover named Sievers, she would probably be ready to become our friend. 'Number 70' therefore throws out this suggestion, yet at the same time impresses upon you and your friends the necessity of the creation of the epidemic and the bringing in of Roumania on the side of the Allies."

Those final words of that cipher despatch disclose a cunning that was indeed unequalled. I know full well that readers may be inclined to pause and to doubt that such dastardly methods could actually be pursued against civilisation. To such I can only point out that boxes of the same microbes were found in the German Legation in Bucharest, and were officially reported by the United States Legation in that city.

The fierce German octopus—so carefully fostered and so well prepared—had alas! stretched its thousand searching tentacles upon the patriotic Russian people who were ruled by their weak and careless Emperor, while the pro-German Empress listened to every rumour, and in her heart hoped for a separate peace with Germany as the only salvation of her land. Truly the Romanoffs have proved themselves a weak-kneed and irresponsible dynasty. Alexander, however, was never weak. In the long-ago days when I had audience with his late Majesty one morning in his small reception-room in the Winter Palace, he wore a rough drab shooting suit; bluff and full-bearded as any of his ministers, he talked to me fully of his regret that the Nihilists should be ever plotting to kill him, and assured me of his own personal efforts to free his people from a corrupt Church and an iron bureaucracy.

"Please tell your British people that as Tsar I am doing the utmost in my power to improve and civilise my dear Russian people, to whom I am devoted, and to whom I will if necessary give my life."

Those words of the father of the Tsar Nicholas will be found reproduced in the columns of *The Times* after my joining as "Russian Correspondent."

But let us examine the result of the secret order to Rasputin from Berlin which I have reproduced above.

In the first place I find among the papers, a letter dated from the Potemkinskaya, 29, as follows:

> Holy Father,
>
> I thank you for your introduction yesterday to Her Majesty the Empress, and to the Grand Duchess Olga. Truly we are all your kindred spirits and disciples, who know at last the joys and pleasures of the life which Almighty God has given unto us. Anna was most charming, and I saw His Majesty as arranged. At your suggestion I mentioned the Gospodin Sievers, and the Emperor has promised to appoint him Vice-Governor of Omsk. All thanks to you, dear Holy Father. I shall be at our reunion at your house to-morrow, and my daughter Nada, who is in search of the Truth, will accompany me. Till then, I kiss your dear hand.
>
> Vera Kokoskin

This letter speaks for itself. Another document is a letter to Rasputin dated from the Hotel Metropole, Moscow, and is in plain language as follows:

> "The consignment of fruit from your generous donors has duly reached the Maison Yakowleff and is being distributed in various charitable quarters and is much appreciated in these days when prices are so high. Some of it has been sent to the

director of the Borgoroditsky Convent at Kazan, and also some to the Society of St. George at Kiev. Please inform and thank the donors.

Karl Johnke

Eagerly the camarilla awaited the result of their dastardly handiwork. The allotted three weeks passed, but no epidemic was reported. Evidently the monk wrote to the German bacteriologist, who was posing as a Dane, for the latter wrote from the Hotel Continental at Kiev:

"The fruit, owing to delays in transit, was not in a condition for human consumption. This is extremely regrettable after all the trouble of our kind donors."

Therefore, while certain isolated cases of cholera were reported from several cities—as the sanitary records prove—Russia had had indeed a providential escape from a terrible epidemic, the infected fruit being distributed over a wide area by charitable organisations quite unsuspicious of its source.

Failure to produce the desired result induced Rasputin and his paymasters in Berlin to adopt yet another method of forcing Russia into a separate peace.

Brusiloff had recommenced his gallant offensive, and the situation was being viewed with increased apprehension by the German General Staff. Roumania was still undecided whether or not to throw in her cause with that of the Allies. The great plot to destroy Roumania is again revealed by documentary evidence contained among Rasputin's papers, and also in the despatches received in Bucharest—where, of course, the clever intrigue was never suspected.

A message in cipher received by Rasputin, on August 8th, the day of General Letchitzki's great triumph, reveals a truly Machiavellian plan. It reads thus:

Memorandum 27546.112

"Matters in the Dobroudja are approaching a serious crisis. Urge S. (Boris Sturmer, the Prime Minister) to suggest at once to the Emperor, while at the same time you make a similar suggestion to Her Majesty, that Roumania must be forced to take up arms against us. She must not be allowed to remain neutral any longer. S. must send a despatch to Bucharest so worded that it is our ultimatum. If she does not join the Allies immediately she must fight against Russia."

Accordingly, three days later, after the Holy Father and his unholy fellow-conspirator had had audiences at Tsarskoe-Selo, Sturmer sent an urgent despatch to the Roumanian Government demanding that it should join the Allies, without further delay. At Bucharest no plot was suspected, and indeed on the face of things, it seemed no unusual request. Even people in Great Britain were daily asking each other "When will Roumania come in it?"

The reason she had not joined was because she was not yet prepared. Germany knew that and with Rasputin's aid had laid a plot to invade her. She was, while still unready, forced into the war by Sturmer. Nineteen days after the despatch of that cipher message from Berlin she formally declared hostilities against Austria-Hungary.

Berlin was delighted, and the sinister "dark force" of Russia rubbed his dirty hands with delight. The plot he saw must succeed. Truly it was a vile and devilish one, which not even the shrewdest diplomat suspected, namely, to deliver Roumania and her resources of grain and oil to the enemy. As an outcome of the conspiracy the Russo-Roumanian army, owing to treachery in the latter, at once retreated under pressure from Mackensen's forces, and very quickly, almost before the Allies were aware of it, Roumania and the Constanza railway were in the enemy's hands. Disaster, engineered by the camarilla, followed disaster after that "Now or never" ultimatum of Sturmer's. The promises made to the brave Roumanians were broken one after the other. Why? Because with Rasputin, Protopopoff and certain Generals suborned by the mock-monk, the Prime Minister's intention was to use the great retreat and the rapid absorption of Roumania as a means to force the Tsar and his Empire into a separate peace.

Indeed, Rasputin—in attendance daily at Tsarskoe-Selo—by declaring to the Empress and his sister-disciples at Court that he had been accorded a vision of the Tsar and Kaiser fraternising, and interpreting this as a divine direction that peace should at once be made with Germany, had very nearly induced His Majesty to sign a declaration of peace, when one man in the Empire discovered the dastardly manoeuvre, the Deputy Gospodin Miliukoff, whose actions I will describe in a further chapter.

VIII

The Mock-Monk Unmasked

Documentary evidence contained in the papers which the monk so carefully preserved shows conclusively that he paid a secret visit to Berlin in the first week of October, 1916. While the brave Russian army were fighting valiantly, ever and anon being betrayed by their leaders, treachery of the worst and vilest sort was afoot in the highest quarters.

That German potentate, the Duke of Mecklenburg-Strelitz, who occupied an important position in the entourage of the Tsar, was acting as counsellor to the Tsaritza, and at the same time, aided actively by the woman Vyrubova, was working to delude the Emperor and defeat his gallant armies. At Russian Field Headquarters the Tsar was cheered everywhere, and his officers were enthusiastic. It was known that the German offensive had spent itself, and it was believed by those who were being bamboozled that, when all was ready, Russia would press on to her well-deserved victory.

But the day of Russia's great offensive never arrived. Great Britain and France were supplying her with guns and munitions conveyed up to Alexandrovsk with much difficulty, and the Allies were daily hoping that the "Russian steam-roller" would once again start upon its westward course. London, Paris and Rome were in ignorance of the amazing plot of the pro-German traitors.

Meanwhile the mock-monk, in the garb of a Dutch pastor, had arrived in Berlin to make arrangements with the enemy for Russia's final conquest.

By the scoundrel's fatal weakness for preserving letters addressed to him, in the hope that when he fell out of favour at Court he might use them for blackmailing purposes—for after all this "holy" man had started life as a common thief—we have again evidence of his treachery in the following letter dated from Tsarskoe-Selo, October 18th, the day following the Allied landing in Athens. Addressed to Rasputin, it is in German, in the fine handwriting of the Tsaritza, and reads as follows:

Holy Father,
 At last we have welcome news of you! This morning your messenger reached us bringing me a letter, and one

for Anna. What you tell us is indeed good news. We are glad that you have seen William (the Emperor), and that he has been so gracious to you. Your news regarding the forthcoming offensive against the British is most encouraging. The British are Germany's real enemies. Tell His Majesty that all goes well, and that Sturmer quite agrees that we must have a separate peace and is taking every step towards that end.

"Nikki is still at the front encouraging the troops. How foolish, and yet we have all to show a bold front. The news of the landing at Athens has disconcerted us, though it has caused great joy in Petrograd. Inquire if nothing can be done further in an attempt to spread disease in the more populous regions. This would kill enthusiasm for the war and force peace quickly.

"Dmitri (the Grand Duke Dmitri Pavlovitch, who was Rasputin's fiercest enemy) has been sent by Nikki to Samara. It would be a relief to us all if he never returned. He with Nicholas (the Grand Duke Nicholas Michailovitch) are plotting to defeat us. But Germany shall win. It shall be as you, my dear Father, saw in your vision.

"Pray for us, O Father. Give us your benediction, for while you are absent we are all dull and lonely. Tell William to send you back quickly and safely to us. Give my best greetings to the brave Hindenburg. It is horrid to be compelled to sustain an anti-German attitude when one knows that our Fatherland is unconquerable, even though the Russian flag be bathed in blood.

"Inform the General Staff that the secret agent Erbach-Furstenau, who fell into General Neudorff's hands last month has at my instigation been acquitted by the court-martial and will very shortly escape back to Germany. I have personally arranged that the papers seized upon him shall be destroyed.

"Charges are being levelled against General Sukhomlinoff. He has been betrayed by a man named Kartzoff. In order to suppress the latter's further activity, he has been arrested for treason at my instigation and sent without trial to an unknown destination. So we have one enemy the less. It is reported that Manasevitch-Manuiloff (private secretary to Prime Minister Sturmer) has been arrested for attempting to blackmail his chief. But I will see that Nikki stops the trial.

"My dear boy Alexis is improving. Anna is with him constantly. He sends his greetings and asks for your prayers. I kiss your holy hand.

Your sister

Alec

Russia was still being betrayed by the Empress, who had fallen so entirely beneath the occult influences of the rascal who, in turn, had become the catspaw of the Kaiser.

The charges against General Sukhomlinoff, ex-Minister of War, mentioned by the Tsaritza, had apparently alarmed her. And well they might. An official in the ministry named Kartzoff had betrayed his chief, whereupon Colonel Tugen Baranovsky, late Chief of the Mobilisation Department of the Russian General Staff, had made depositions to the effect that the mobilisation plans drafted by the General were full of errors, while rifles, machine-guns, and field and heavy guns were all lacking. Depositions had been made by General Petrovsky, late Chief of the Fortifications Department, to the effect that the General had only twice visited the artillery administration during the whole time he held his portfolio as Minister, while a third official, Colonel Batvinkine, one of the heads of the Artillery Administration, had asserted that General Sukhomlinoff had insisted upon important contracts for machine-guns being given to the Rickerts Factory at a cost of two thousand roubles each while the Toula Factory could turn out excellent machine-guns at nine hundred roubles.

Such were a few of the charges against the ex-Minister, a bosom friend of Rasputin and of Sturmer, and these were being whispered abroad everywhere, even though by the influence of the Tsaritza the principal witness against the General had been sent to "an unknown destination!"

Written on the same day and conveyed secretly to the monk in Berlin—evidently by the same messenger who carried the Tsaritza's letter to her "Holy Father"—was one from the conspirator Protopopoff. It is on the private note-paper of the Minister of the Interior and discloses truly an amazing state of affairs, as follows:

Brother Gregory,

I send you this hastily and with some apprehension. Both Nicholas and Dmitri (the Grand Dukes), are actively at work against us! Beware! They know far too much, hence it behoves us to be most discreet. I was at Tsarskoe-Selo yesterday and discussed it with F. (Count Fredericks, Minister of the Imperial Court). There is a secret movement to upset our plans, but I have ordered the Secret Police to spare no pains to present full and adequate reports to me, and rely on me to take drastic steps.

"An hour ago it came to my knowledge that an individual named Wilhelm Gebhardt, living at Hildegard-strasse, 21 Wilmersdorf, Berlin, has knowledge that you are in the German capital and is probably watching your movements to report to our enemies here. Give news of this to our friend 'Number 70' and urge that he shall be immediately arrested as a spy of Russia. If he is executed his mouth would be closed, for he is dangerous. The man with whom he is in association in Petrograd, a person named Tchartovyski, member of the Duma, I have ordered to be arrested and charged with communicating with persons in Germany.

"S. (Sturmer) is eager for news regarding the proposed German offensive against the British in Flanders, and the exact position regarding the 'U' boat campaign. Inform the Chancellor that news we received from Washington to-day shows that President Wilson is determined, and warn him that J. and G., whom he will know by initials as German agents in the United States, have been discovered, and may be arrested. He may perhaps communicate with them by wireless, and they may escape while there is still time.

"Further, inform the Chancellor that our efforts to make more marked the shortage of food have been negatived by the action of Nicholas and Dmitri, for we fear to go further lest the truth be disclosed. Their activity cannot be ignored.

"Urge that the distribution of fruit to charitable institutions be repeated.

"The charges against Sukhomlinoff are extremely grave, and may have serious consequences. I am, however, taking steps to ascertain the intentions and to arrest those who are in association.

"Her Majesty is eager and nervous regarding you. Write and assure her that all is well with your dear self. As the saviour of Russia from the wiles of the Allies, the Russian people ought to regard you as great as the Great Peter himself.

"A tall, thin individual named Emil Dollen will probably call upon you at your hotel. If so, receive him. He may convey a message from me sent by wireless to Riga and re-transmitted.

"Present my humble compliments to His Majesty the Emperor. Would that I were with you at glorious Potsdam. These Russians of ours are arrant fools, or we should have been hand-in-glove with Berlin against the effete nations who are our Allies. I salute you and await your return.

Your brother,
D.A. Protopopoff

This autograph letter is from the man who was Russian Minister of the Interior—the man in whom every true-born son of Russia believed so implicitly that he went to his death fiercely and gallantly for his Emperor!

Surely that position had no parallel in history. Imperial Germany with her long-prepared plans had seized the Russian bear by the throat, and was throttling it, just as she has attempted to grapple with the British lion. If the ever-spreading tentacles of the Kaiser's propaganda bureau and his unscrupulous and well-financed spy-service were so successful in Russia, which before the war was half-Germanised by the Tsaritza, the villain Rasputin and their traitor ministers, then one is permitted to wonder to what depths the Koniggratzer-strasse, with the Kaiser at its head, have descended in order to try and create famine and revolution in the British Isles, wherein dwell "the worst enemies of Germany."

The documentary evidence extant shows that the unkempt "prophet," whose peasant hands were kissed by the Empress of Russia, and before whom bowed the greatest ladies of the Imperial Court, lived during the greater part of October, 1916, in that small hotel, the Westfalischer-Hof, in the Neusladische-strasse, on the north of the Linden. He called himself Pastor van Meeuwen, and his companion was his trusty manservant, a cosmopolitan fellow, who afterwards disclosed much that I have here been able to reveal to British readers.

That he had frequent audiences of the Emperor William and received his personal instructions is apparent from the copies of telegrams which the revolutions eventually unearthed from the archives of the Ministry of Telegraphs.

One message by wireless, despatched from a Russian warship in the Baltic to the Admiralty station at Reval, coded in the same cipher as that used by Rasputin and his German confederates, the key of which was found in the safe in the Gorokhovaya, is as follows:

To his Excellency the Minister Protopopoff

All goes well. I had an audience at the Neues Palais to-day of three hours' duration. Inform Charles Michael (the Duke Charles Michael of Mecklenburg-Strelitz, who was the German adviser of the Tsaritza, and naturalised as a Russian subject in July, 1914) that the Emperor William sends his best greetings and acknowledgments of his despatch of the 3rd inst. It has been found necessary to recall the troops who have been held ready at Hamburg and Bremen for the invasion of Britain. The General Staff have, after due consideration, decided that an invasion might meet with disaster, hence they are turning their attention to submarine and aerial attacks upon Britain in order to crush her. I have learnt from a conversation with the Kaiser that London is to be destroyed by a succession of fleets of super-aeroplanes launching newly-devised explosive and poison-gas bombs of a terribly destructive character.

"Urge S. (Sturmer) to disclaim at once all knowledge of the Rickert contracts. The payments are completely concealed. I have no fear of Sukhomlinoff's betrayal. He is discredited and will not be believed: yet it would be best if the Emperor ordered the trial to be cancelled.—The Tsar did so, but the General was tried after his deposition.

"To yourself and our dear Empress greetings. I pray for you all, and send you my benedictions.

Your brother,
Gregory Efimovitch

That the rascal hurried back to Petrograd is apparent by a letter dated a week later from Madame Kokoskin, the latest of his sister-disciples, who wrote from the Potemkinskaya 29, Petrograd, saying:

Holy Father,

I have just heard with joy from dear Anna that you have returned to-night. May God grant you the fruits of your pilgrimage. (To his sister-disciples he had pretended to make a pilgrimage to the monastery of Verkhotursky, where in secret most disgraceful orgies often took place.) My daughter Nada will be with me at our reunion at Anna's to-morrow at six.

Vera

Rasputin seems to have arrived in Petrograd the bearer of certain verbal messages from the Kaiser to the Tsaritza, for he went at once to Tsarskoe-Selo and there remained all next day. That the Empress had now grown very frightened regarding the attitude of the Grand Dukes Nicholas and Dmitri, the latter a young and energetic figure in Russian politics, is proved by an attempt which, a few days later, she made to conciliate them both. But they discarded her advances, for, having already learnt much regarding the "Holy Father," they were actively preparing to bring about the prosecution of General Sukhomlinoff, well knowing that its disclosures must wreck the *regime* of the hated mock-monk and shake the House of Romanoff to its foundations.

Hence it was that, two days later, the patriotic informer Ivan Kartzoff, the unfortunate official who had been sent by the Tsaritza's influence to "an unknown destination," was found shot dead in a wood near Kislovodsk, a small town in the North Caucasus, while two of the other witnesses were arrested at Protopopoff's orders upon false charges of treachery, incriminating papers—which had been placed among their effects by *agents provocateurs*—being produced as evidence against them.

Thus the most strenuous efforts were being made by the camarilla to prevent the bursting of that storm-cloud which grew darker over them with every day that passed.

The monk was, however, fully alive to the danger of exposure, and he therefore resolved to play yet another bold clever card in the desperate game of the betrayal of the Russian nation.

IX

Documentary Evidence of Treachery

G ermany never plays straight, even with those who accept her gold to play the dangerous game of traitor. The few who know the ramifications of the underground politics of Europe are well aware of this fact.

This was brought home to Rasputin, when immediately after his return to Petrograd from his secret visit to the Kaiser in the guise of a pious Dutch pastor, the German Press became guilty of a grave indiscretion. Naturally the monk waxed furious. The *Kolnische Zeitung*, in its unwonted enthusiasm, wrote: "We Germans need have no fear. Sturmer may be relied upon not to place any obstacles in the way of Russia's desire for peace with Germany." While the *Reichspost* said: "We may rest assured that Sturmer will be independent in his relations with Downing Street."

And yet Sturmer was at this moment crying, "No separate peace!" and had sent constant despatches to Downing Street assuring us of his intention to prosecute the war to the finish. By this he misled the Allies, who naturally regarded the assertion of the German newspapers as mere frothy enthusiasm.

But those indiscreet German assurances were instantly seized upon by that small and fearless band of Russian patriots who—headed by the Grand Dukes Nicholas and Dmitri—had united to expose and destroy the disgraceful camarilla whose object it was to wreck the Empire, and hand it mangled and defenceless to be torn by the eagle of Germany.

At the instigation of the peasant-charlatan and thief whose hand the Empress kissed, calling him her Holy Father, Sturmer—also paid lavishly by Germany—was following a clever policy of isolation, and had raised a lofty barrier between the Government and the elected representatives of the people. After ten months of office this *debauchee* and traitor had only appeared in the Duma on one occasion, and then he made a speech so puerile that he was greeted with ironical laughter.

With the very refinement of cunning which betrayed the criminal mind, he, at Rasputin's suggestion, crowded the work of legislation into the Parliamentary recesses, and passed Bills by virtue of Article 87 of the Fundamental Laws, which allowed the Government to legislate when the Duma was not in session. Till then all had gone smoothly for Berlin. But there opened a new chapter of the history of the downfall of the great Romanoffs.

Early in November, 1916, a number of very serious and secret conferences of the camarilla took place at Rasputin's house. Both Sturmer and Protopopoff were now viewing the situation with the gravest anxiety, for the Empire was being swiftly aroused to a sense of its insecurity. There were sinister whispers on all hands of traitors, and of a disinclination on the part of the capitalists and Government to win the war.

The Empress had been guilty of a serious indiscretion, for she had mentioned to a young officer at Court the dastardly attempt of German agents to produce an epidemic of cholera by distribution of infected fruit to charitable institutions. That officer's name was Tsourikoff. The hand of Rasputin was heavy and swift. Four days after the fact became known he died suddenly in his rooms in the Moskovskaya Quarter in Petrograd. He had been to the Bouffes in the Fontanka, where he had met a dark-eyed siren with whom he had afterwards had supper at that well-known establishment, Pivato's, in the Morskaya. The lady could not be traced after his death. Truly the hand of the illiterate monk was ruling Russia with his pretence of working miracles, and with that mock-religious jargon in which he addressed his noble-born sister-disciple. He held secret death within his fingers, to be dealt to any who might upset his plans, or those of the Empress.

That the latter actually did, in an excess of her enthusiasm for the success of her native Germany, betray the plans of Rasputin and his paymasters to the young officer Tsourikoff, is proved by a telegram which she addressed to the monk from the Imperial train at Sinelnikovo, on the way to Livadia. This sardonic message still remains upon the records of the Department of Posts and Telegraphs, and reads:

> "The accident to Captain Tsourikoff is to be deplored. Please place a wreath upon the grave on my behalf. Pray for us.
>
> Alec

In the last days of October, 1916, the diabolical conspiracy entered upon a new and even more desperate stage, for very slowly the astounding truth was leaking out to the long-suffering Russian people. The Grand

Duke Nicholas had been joined by the Grand Duke Serge, formerly Inspector-General of Artillery, General Vernandea, ex-Assistant Minister of War, and M. Mimascheff, who all three had been actively investigating the alleged treachery of General Sukhomlinoff. They had publicly made further statements most damning to the General. His late colleague Vernandea had alleged that the Minister of War had paid no heed to the equipment of the Army, had given no contracts except to those factories who gave him bribes, and that after 130 days of war the Russian Army were without shells. The Grand Duke Serge had told a secret meeting in Petrograd that General Sukhomlinoff had suppressed the personal reports addressed to the Tsar by all the heads of the Ministry of War and had actually prevented new guns being ordered from the Schneider Works, while the ex-Minister of Commerce declared that the Minister of War had never once requested him to organise manufacturers and owners of works for national defence.

On hearing from Rasputin that these allegations were being made, the Empress at once, at the monk's instigation, telegraphed in cipher to the Tsar, who was at the front:

> "Suppress at once, I beg of you in the interest of us all, the
> base charges now being made against Sukhomlinoff. Boris
> threatens to resign if they continue. If you do not act
> immediately the situation will become a very ugly one."

In reply the Emperor sent a message to his wife at Livadia next day, in which he said:

> "I have taken the necessary steps that the allegations shall not
> be repeated."

They were, however, repeated in Court at the trial of the ex-Minister at Petrograd on August 28, 1917.

Meanwhile Rasputin, Sturmer, and Protopopoff, a truly diabolical trio, proceeded to put into force a new and ingenious plan to create further unrest and by that means dishearten the people. The Empress returned to Tsarskoe-Selo, where the charlatan immediately saw her and obtained her full approval to his suggestion. The plan was to disseminate the wildest rumours, in order to incite disorder among the proletariat. In that highly-charged atmosphere created by the growing food crisis—which Sturmer and Protopopoff had so cleverly brought about at Germany's instigation—it was easy to throw a spark among the inflammable popular masses, exasperated and disorganised by the deplorable state of affairs. In consequence, a veritable whirlwind of false rumour was released in the hope that a movement would be started which would shatter, weaken for long, or stifle all manifestations of patriotism, and cause the country to sue for a separate peace.

Rasputin himself was responsible for putting this new plan into execution. Rumours arose with a startling rapidity. It was said in Petrograd that all Moscow was involved in a rising; the wires were cut, the Moscow police were on strike, and that the troops had refused to fire on the crowd. Simultaneously, similar rumours were circulated in Moscow concerning a sanguinary riot in Petrograd; while at Kharkoff it was believed that Moscow was in revolution, and at Moscow it was declared that there was a revolution at Kharkoff.

These rumours, which all emanated from the malignant brain of the "Saint," were of course false, but colour was given to them by the dastardly outrages committed by two German secret agents, Lachkarioff and Filimonoff (who were subsequently allowed to escape to Sweden), who blew up two great mills outside Moscow, and also blew up the blast furnaces at the Obukhov Steel Factory, causing great loss of life; while at the same time, a desperate attempt was made also by other German agents to destroy the great powder factory opposite Schusselburg, which, before the war, had been owned by Germans.

The unrest thus created by Rasputin quickly assumed alarming proportions, and the camarilla was secretly satisfied. The Prime Minister, Sturmer, in order to mislead the public further, made a speech deploring the fact that anybody credited such unfounded reports; but he did not do so before the Labour group of the Central War Industrial Committee had issued a declaration to the working classes warning them to remain patient and prosecute the war with vigour.

How amazingly clever was this traitorous camarilla, seeking to hurl Russia to her destruction, is shown by a significant fact. On the very day of the issue of that Labour declaration General Brusiloff, interviewed at the Russian Headquarters of the South-West Front by Mr. Stanley Washburn, said:

"The war is won to-day, though it is merely speculation to estimate how much longer will be required before the enemy are convinced that the cause, for the sake of which they drenched Europe with blood, is irretrievably lost. Personally, never since the beginning have I believed that the enemy had a chance of winning."

Meanwhile the Emperor was still absent at the front, and Rasputin, in addition to directing the affairs of the Empire through the Empress, whom he visited daily at the Palace, was holding constant reunions of his sister-disciples, whereat he pretended to see visions, while he was also blackmailing all and sundry, as his voluminous correspondence with some of his "sisters" plainly shows. Two letters from the Grand Duchess Olga, daughter of the Tsar, dated October 30th and November 1st, are indeed plain evidence that the monk was forming a fresh "circle" of his female neophytes, consisting wholly of young girls of noble families.

Suddenly, like a bombshell, there dropped upon the Tsaritza and the camarilla the startling news, that Miliukoff, who had now at his back the Grand Dukes Nicholas, Serge and Dmitri, intended to publicly expose the Empress's pet "Saint." From Tsarskoe-Selo she wrote to him on November 7th, apparently in great haste, for it is a pencilled note:

> Holy Father,
> Anna has just told me of Miliukoff's intention in the Duma. The Emperor must further adjourn its re-assembling (which had been prohibited from meeting since July). I have telegraphed to him urging him to do this. If not, Noyo's suggestion to pay the agents J. or B. ten thousand roubles to remove him. I would willingly pay a hundred thousand roubles to close his mouth for ever. This must be done. Suggest it to P. (Protopopoff). Surely the same means could be used as with Tsourikoff, and the end be quite natural and peaceful! You could supply the means as before. But I urge on you not to delay a moment. All depends upon Miliukoff's removal. If he reveals to the Duma what he knows, then everything must be lost. I kiss your dear hands. With Olga I ask your blessing.
>
> > Your dutiful daughter,
> > A.

It seems incredible in this twentieth century that an Empress should have been so completely beneath the thraldom of an erotic criminal lunatic. But the evidence is there in black and white.

Two previous attempts upon the life of Professor Miliukoff had happily failed, but the tenor of that letter illustrates the Tsaritza's increasing fears lest the real traitor should be unmasked.

A cipher telegram from the Emperor, who was at the South-West Headquarters, is on record, dated November 8th, and was addressed to the Tsaritza. It was evidently a reply to her frantic request:

> "Tell our dear Father (Rasputin) that to postpone the Duma would, I fear, create an unfavourable impression, and I judge impossible. Protopopoff has asked my authority to arrest Miliukoff upon some technical charge, but I do not consider such a course good policy. I agree that to-day's situation is grave, and agree that at the last moment some steps should be taken to prevent him from speaking."

On receipt of that very unsatisfactory reply the Tsaritza summoned the mock-monk, who was remaining at the Palace evidently awaiting the Emperor's reply. Sturmer and Madame Vyrubova, the high-priestess of the Rasputin cult, were also present. What actually transpired at that Council of Three is unknown. It is, however, beyond question that it was arranged that M. Miliukoff, whom they held in such fear—as well as a friend of his, a Conservative deputy named Puriskevitch—should be "removed." That the illiterate scoundrel, with his unique knowledge of the scriptures, was an adept in the art of using certain secret drugs, and that by his hand several persons obnoxious to the camarilla had died mysteriously is now proved beyond any doubt, for as cleverly as he systematically drugged the poor little Tsarevitch, so also he could with amazing cunning "arrange" the deaths of those who might betray him.

M. Miliukoff, knowing that his patriotic and hostile intentions were being suspected, took such precautions, however, that even the bold emissaries of Rasputin failed to approach him.

At noon, on November 14th, the Minister Protopopoff wrote a hurried note upon the paper of the Ministry of the Interior, which is on record, and is as follows:

> Dear friend Gregory,
>   How is it that your plans have so utterly failed and M. (Miliukoff) is still active? To-day at 2 the Duma meets! Cannot you arrange that he is absent? Cannot you work a

miracle? Skoropadski (a well-known German agent) has betrayed us and put the most incriminating documents into M.'s hands. We tried to arrest the fellow last night in Riga, but, alas, he has eluded us. Take every precaution for your own safety. If M. attends the sitting we are all lost.

Yours cordially,

D.A.P.

The plot to kill M. Miliukoff had failed! The Empress knew of it and sat in the Winter Palace, pale, breathless and eager for messages over her private telephone. The vile, black work done by her "Holy Father" was to be exposed! What if her own Imperial self were exhibited in her true traitorous colours!

Meanwhile, at two o'clock, M. Rodzianko took his seat as President at the Tauris Palace. The usual service was held and then the historic sitting of the Duma opened. The House was crowded, and the British, French and Italian Ambassadors being in the diplomatic box, the members, Octobrists, Progressive Nationalists, the Centre, the Zemsto Octobrists and Cadets, rose in one body and gave vociferous cheers for the Allies. "Russia will win!" they cried.

The first speaker was M. Garusewicz, who, on behalf of the Polish Club, addressed the Allied Powers, protesting against the Austro-German action and expressing the hope and confidence that a final solution of the Polish problem would be the outcome of the war.

The two men whom the camarilla had plotted to murder were calmly in their places. M. Miliukoff, a pleasant-looking grey-haired man, sat gazing at the speaker through his gold-rimmed spectacles, listening attentively until the speaker had concluded. Meanwhile the Tsaritza, sitting in her luxurious little room in the Palace with the dissolute Anna Vyrubova as her sole companion, was listening to messages which, as arranged, came to her over the telephone every ten minutes.

At last M. Miliukoff rose, quite calm, and bowed to the President. Instantly there was silence. Without mincing matters in the least he told the House—in a speech which was wholly suppressed by the authorities—how the camarilla had endeavoured to remove him but in vain; and then, after many hard words which electrified all present, he denounced the "Saint" as the dark and sinister force which was hurling the Russian Empire to its destruction. Then, branding the pro-German Prime Minister Boris Sturmer as "Judas the Traitor," he took up a bundle of documents, and shaking them in his hand dramatically he declared: "I have here, gentlemen, the evidence of Judas. Evidence in cold figures—the number of shekels, the pieces of silver, for betrayal."

The House sat breathless! The ghastly truth was out. When M. Miliukoff sat down his friend M. Puriskevitch rose politely and asked permission and indulgence to make a speech in German—the hated language—promising it should be very brief. All he uttered were the two words: "Hofmeister Sturmer!" The Duma, understanding, cheered to the echo.

Over the telephone the Empress, pale and neurotic, listened to what had been alleged against her "Holy Father" and his friend Sturmer, whereupon she suddenly gave a low scream and fainted.

The truth was out at last! The first blow of retribution had on that afternoon fallen upon the Imperial House of Romanoff.

But Rasputin, the amazing, remained unperturbed. He merely smiled evilly. The game had become desperate, he knew, but he still had other cards to play.

X

DISCLOSES THE CHARLATAN'S WILES

U p till this juncture the penalty for even mentioning the name of Rasputin was imprisonment. The censorship, controlled by his catspaw Protopopoff, took care to adopt the most drastic measures to suppress every mention of the mysterious "Saint" who was the centre of that band of neurotic noblewomen who kissed his filthy hands and bowed their knees to him.

"O Holy Father! the Chosen One of God! Give us thy blessing and we beseech of thee to pray for us. May the sin we here commit be committed for the purification of our souls; and may we, thy sister-disciples, be raised to thine own plane of piety by God's great mercy."

Thus ran the blasphemous opening prayer repeated at each of the scoundrel's erotic reunions—those meetings held with closed doors both within the Palace of Tsarskoe-Selo, in the Gorokhovaya, and elsewhere.

But on that historic November 14th, 1916, the "Saint" had been publicly named, and hence became seriously alarmed. Two hours after the fearless Miliukoff had denounced him in the Duma the whole of Petrograd palpitated with excitement. All knew that the utterances of the fearless patriot who had actually pilloried the monk in public would be denied publication in the Press. Therefore those who were bent upon winning the war at once arranged to have typewritten copies of the speech circulated from hand to hand, and by that means the bold denunciation obtained a wider circulation than any other words ever spoken in the Duma.

The newspapers appeared with black columns. "M. Miliukoff continued the debate," was all that was allowed to appear in print. The cables to the Allies were rigorously censored, so that in England even Downing Street were in ignorance of what had really occurred. Paris, London and Rome were still living in a fool's paradise, thanks to the grip which Germany had gained upon official Petrograd, and were being led to believe that all in the Russian Empire were united against the hated Hun.

The reports in the British Press of that period were most mystifying. That the Duma were dissatisfied with the state of affairs was plain, but had not the House of Commons often expressed equal dissatisfaction? The fact, however, that the name of Rasputin had actually been mentioned and that the "Holy Father" had been exposed as Germany's spy, who controlled the "Hofmeister Sturmer," was never dreamed until a month later, even by such outspoken journals as the Paris *Matin*.

At Tsarskoe-Selo, however, all were in deadly fear. Even Anna Vyrubova viewed the situation with greatest alarm. She wrote to him an hour after Miliukoff had denounced him, as follows:

> "Her Majesty is prostrated. All seems lost. The Emperor departs for the front again at midnight. He fears a rising in Petrograd, and is regretful that M. (Miliukoff) was not suppressed in time to save us. Someone, he says, has blundered. If you would save yourself go instantly upon a pilgrimage. Describe a vision that will allay the people's anger and give them further confidence in you. M. has denounced you as a mocker of God and a mere juggler with woman's credulity. Our dear Empress knows you are not. But she must continue in that belief. Shall Alexis be taken with another seizure? If so, prophesy the day and hour. I await word from you in secret, and ask your blessing.
>
> Your sister,
Anna

The suggestion in this letter is, of course, that a dose of the secret drug be administered to the poor little Tsarevitch at an hour to be previously prophesied by the mock-monk. The Matter was, however, on the alert. On receipt of the letter he went at once to the Palace, abruptly leaving the camarilla who had assembled to plot further, and to save themselves and their own fat emoluments by more juggling with the security of the Empire.

To the Empress, whom he found in her *neglige* in her boudoir, with Anna in sole attendance, he said:

> "Truly, O Sister! our enemies seek to encompass us! But God is our strength. As surely as the Russian people have

denounced me, so surely will God in His wrath send His punishment upon the Heir to the Throne. Miliukoff, who has sought the protection of Satan himself, has spoken his poisonous words against me. Therefore I go to-morrow upon a pilgrimage to retire and to pray for the future of the Empire, and the forgiveness of those who have dared to speak ill of one sent by God as the Deliverer."

"No! No!" gasped Her Majesty, starting from her chair in pale alarm. "You will not leave us at this juncture—you will not, Holy Father, leave us to our fate?"

"It is decreed," he said in that low hard voice of his. "I have witnessed a vision even an hour since—I have heard the Voice! I must obey. But," he added seriously, "I tell thee, O Sister! that near five o'clock in the morning of the day following to-morrow thy dear son will be visited by God's wrath. He—"

"He will be again ill!" gasped the unhappy woman, who believed that the bearded man in the black kaftan before her was sent by Providence as Russia's deliverer. "Surely you cannot mean that! You will pray for him—you will save him. Remember he is my son—my all!"

"Truly I mean what I have spoken, O Sister!" was his reply. "But I will pray for his recovery—and all can be achieved by the sacrifice of the flesh and by prayer. God grant his recovery!" he added piously, making the sign of the cross and raising his mesmeric eyes heavenwards.

At this the hysterical traitress in her pale-pink gown edged with wide Eastern embroidery of emeralds and turquoises, fell upon her knees and kissed the scoundrel's knotted, unclean fingers, while her faithful Anna looked on and crossed herself, muttering one of the prayers in the blasphemous jargon of the "sister-disciples." The failure to assassinate Professor Miliukoff had brought home to the camarilla and also to the spy-bureau in Berlin—acting through Swedish diplomatic channels—that the Grand Dukes Nicholas, Serge and Dmitri, together with their small circle of staunch friends of the nobility, were determined to place them in the pillory.

The agent of Germany, Skoropadski, a friend of the notorious Azeff, of the Russian Secret Police, whose exploits before the war were often chronicled, had betrayed his employers. Commencing life as a Russian *agent provocateur*, employed in Warsaw against the Revolutionists, and consequently a most unscrupulous and heartless person, he had entered the service of Germany with Protopopoff's connivance and had been the means of the ruin and downfall of dozens of patriotic Russian officials. By virtue of his office as spy of Germany he knew the double game that the Prime Minister, Sturmer, was playing at Rasputin's instigation. Documents passed through his hands, and often he passed in secret between Petrograd and Berlin and *vice versa*, posing as a Swede and travelling by way of Stockholm.

He was an expert spy, and ready to serve any paymaster. Furthermore, he had a grudge against Rasputin because one of his own lady friends had joined the cult of "Believers," and thus had his hatred been aroused. Therefore, when the little band of patriots at the head of which was the Grand Duke Nicholas approached him in secret, he was at once ready to place the most damning documentary evidence in their hands—those papers which Professor Miliukoff had flashed in the faces of the Duma.

The anger of Sturmer and Protopopoff was now at a white heat. The latter, as Controller of the Secret Police, made every effort to arrest the artful Pole, but he happily escaped, and is now believed to be in Paris.

Such was the story, revealed here for the first time, of the manner in which the Revolutionists were able to present to the people's representative the infamous acts of the monk Rasputin and his official "creatures" who wore their tinselled uniforms, their tin decorations and enjoyed titles of "Excellency." Traitors have been in every land since the Creation; and, as I examined this amazing *dossier* collected by the patriotic party in Russia, with its original letters, its copies of letters, its photographs and its telegrams in the sloped calligraphy of their senders, I marvel, and wonder who in other countries are the traitors—who while pretending to serve their own kings or their presidents are also serving the Mammon of Germania?

I pen these chapters of the downfall of Tsardom with unwilling hand, for I have many friends in Russia and, as a traveller in the Land of the Tsar over many thousands of versts, I have grown to know— perhaps only slightly—the hearty, homely and hospitable Russian people. I have suffered discomforts for months among those clouds of mosquitoes on the great "tundra," and I have travelled many and many weary miles over the snows of winter, yet never did I think that I should sit to chronicle such a *debacle*.

Notwithstanding the tears of the Empress, the villainous Rasputin, having arranged with Anna the hour when she should drug the poor little Tsarevitch, departed on a pilgrimage to the Monastery of Tsarytsine.

Facts concerning this journey, when he fled from the wrath of the people, have just been revealed by his friend the monk Helidor, who having learnt the manner in which he betrayed the Empire, has come forward to elucidate many things hitherto mysterious.

Helidor, who is a man of high intelligence and true religious principles, has stated that at Rasputin's invitation both he and Monsignor Hermogene joined "Grichka," as he terms his dissolute friend, upon the pilgrimage. Rasputin the traitor was received everywhere as an angel from Heaven. The people of all classes prostrated themselves and kissed his unclean hands. In Tsarytsine during two days he entered many houses, where he embraced all the good-looking women, but discarded the old and ugly. He was often drunk and riotous.

On entering the monastery at last he isolated himself for four days on pretence of prayer, but he was assisted in his religious exercises by a good-looking young nun with whom he openly walked in the monastery grounds.

Tired of the retirement and the nun's companionship, he travelled to his native Siberian village of Pokrovsky, Helidor accompanying him.

"During our journey, which was a long one," Helidor says, "I tried to discover some testimony to the sanctity of my companion. I only found him to be a most uncouth and dissolute person, whose constant talk was of women, and who drank incessantly. I had been mystified by him until then, but I realised that even having been denounced in the Duma, he was quite undisturbed, for his egotism was colossal, and he constantly declared to me that he was the actual Autocrat."

Helidor's description of the so-called "monastery" at Pokrovsky is interesting as being from an authentic and reliable source.

"We arrived there at last," he declared in an interview the other day. "It was a mean Siberian village half hidden in the Siberian snow, for the winter was unduly early. I observed my host closely, for I now knew him to be a traitor and a charlatan. The 'monastery' as he called it in Petrograd, and for which hundreds gave him subscriptions, was not a religious house at all, and it had never been consecrated as such. Rasputin himself was not even a monk, for he had never been received into the church."

In describing this "monastery" for which the monk had filched thousands upon thousands of roubles from the pockets of his neophytes in Petrograd, Helidor says:

"It was a large house, which had only recently been furnished luxuriously. It was full of holy ikons, of portraits of women, and of magnificent presents from their Majesties. The occupants of the place numbered a dozen women, mostly young, garbed as nuns and performing daily religious observances."

Apparently the establishment was a Siberian "Abode of Love," much upon the lines, as the Smyth-Piggott cult, yet Helidor has declared that what struck him most was the open hostility of the mujiks towards the "Holy Father."

"They are annoyed, my dear brother Helidor, because you have come with me from Petrograd," the "saint" declared in excuse.

But Helidor noticed that Antoine, the Archbishop of Tobolsk, who visited him, betrayed the same marked hostility, while the people of the village all declared without mincing matters that Grichka, whom they had known as a convicted horse-thief and assaulter of women, was merely a *debauche*.

Again came wild telegrams from the Empress. The "Saint's" prophecy had been fulfilled and the Tsarevitch had been taken seriously ill at the exact hour he had predicted.

"Nikki has returned. Both of us are in deadly fear," she telegraphed. "Kousmin (the Court physician) cannot diagnose the malady. Come to us at once, Holy Father, I pray to you, come and save us. Give your blessing and your sympathy to your devoted sister.—A."

At the same time His Majesty sent a telegraphic message to the man who made and unmade Ministers and who ruled all Russia at home and in the field. It was despatched from the Winter Palace half-an-hour after the message of the Empress, and read:

Friend,

I cannot command, but I beg of you to return instantly to us. We want your help. Without it, Alexis will die, and the House of Romanoff is doomed. I have sent the Imperial train to you. It leaves in an hour.

Nicholas

Of this summons the villainous ex-thief took no notice.

Helidor says: "He showed me the telegrams and laughed triumphantly, saying, 'Nikki seems very much troubled! Why does he not return to the front and urge on his soldiers against the advancing hosts.' The greater our losses the nearer shall we be to peace. I shall take care that ignorant Russia will not win against the causes of civilisation and humanity."

"Civilisation and humanity!" This illiterate and dissolute peasant, who each night became hopelessly intoxicated and who in his cups would revile his paymasters the Huns and chant in his deep bass voice refrains of Russian patriotic airs, was actually the dear "friend" of the Tsar of All the Russias! The vicious scoundrel's influence was reaching its zenith.

To Western readers the whole facts may well appear incredible. But those who know Russia, with its complex world of official corruption and "religious" chicanery, are well aware how anything may happen to that huge Empire when at war.

After a fortnight's silence, during which the sinister hand of Anna Vyrubova regularly administered that secret drug to the poor, helpless son of the Emperor, Rasputin, with amazing effrontery, dared again to put his foot in Petrograd. On the night of his arrival the Tsaritza, awaiting him anxiously at Tsarskoe-Selo, sent him a note by Ivan Radzick, the trusted body-servant of the Emperor for fifteen years, a note which the miracle-worker preserved most carefully, and which ran as follows:

Holy Father,

I await you eagerly. Boris (Sturmer) and Fredericks are with me. Things are increasingly critical. Hasten to us at once and cure poor little Alexis, or he will die. The doctors are powerless. I have had urgent news from Berlin. Miliukoff must be removed, and so must Kerensky and Nicholas (the Grand Duke). Boris has arranged it. You have the means. Something must happen to them within the next forty-eight hours. Nicholas has handed Nikki an abominable letter of threats. The British Ambassador is wary and knows of this. His despatches to London to-night must be intercepted. I am sending the car for you, and await in eagerness once again to kiss your dear hands.

Your devoted sister,
Alec

XI

BAMBOOZLING THE ALLIES

As a result of the denunciation in the Duma of "Russia's dark forces," Boris Sturmer was deprived of the Premiership and appointed by the Tsaritza's influence to a high office in the Imperial household, where he could still unite with Baron Fredericks in playing Germany's game.

A few days after this re-shuffling of the cards, M. Trepoff, the new Premier, made a reassuring statement to the Duma, in which he said: "There will never be a premature or separate peace. Nothing can change this resolution, which is the inflexible will of the august Russian sovereign, who stands for the whole of his faithful people."

How Rasputin and the camarilla must have chuckled when they read these words of reassurance!

On the very day that declaration was made the monk had received a telegram in cipher from Stockholm, whither it had been first sent from the Koniggratzer-strasse in Berlin, and which, de-coded, reads as follows:

> "Gregersen (a well-known German agent who had actively assisted von Papen in America) is arriving at Archangel upon a munition ship from New York. You will have early news of him. See that he is placed under P.'s (Protopopoff's) protection. He will bring you four boxes. Do not open them, but see they are stored carefully. Hand them to our friend R. (Professor Rogovitch, of Samara, a bacteriologist and friend of Rasputin).
>
> Number 70

The monk had "early news" of the arrival of the spy Gregersen, for on the day following the receipt of that advice of his coming, the ship upon which he had travelled from New York blew up in Archangel harbour, and no fewer than one thousand, eight hundred persons were killed or injured! Gregersen arrived at the Gorokhovaya that same night, and there met Protopopoff, who furnished him with false papers, upon which his photograph was pasted and sealed.

The four wooden boxes which the spy had brought from America, and which contained the bacilli of anthrax and bubonic plague, were, two days later, handed by the monk to the Professor. But the latter, carelessly handling them when opening them, became infected with anthrax himself, and subsequently died in great agony. By the scoundrel's timely death Russia was spared an epidemic of those two terrible diseases, it being the intention of Rogovitch and Rasputin to infect with plague the rats in Moscow and other cities.

The fact can never, of course, be disguised that the Tsar was fully cognisant of Rasputin's evil influence at the Imperial Court, though it seems equally certain that he never suspected him to be the arch-plotter and creature of the Kaiser that he really was. Before the war, Nicholas II had lived a hermit's life at Tsarskoe-Selo. Every foreign diplomat who has been stationed in Petrograd since his accession knows that he was the echo of everyone's opinion except his own. The flexibility of his mind was only equalled by its emptiness. Personal in everything, weak, shallow-minded, yet well-intentioned, he had long been interested in spiritualistic seances and table-turning. Indeed, the most notorious frauds and charlatans who brought psychical studies into disrepute have had the honour of "performing" before His Majesty, and have even received decorations from the hands of the gulled Emperor. It is, therefore, not surprising that this bold and amazingly cunning Siberian peasant known as "Grichka," with his mock miracles—worked by means of drugs supplied to him by the fellow Badmayeff, another charlatan who represented himself as an expert upon "Thibetan" medicine and who had a large clientele in Petrograd society—could so gull the Emperor that he actually consulted "the Holy Father" upon the most important matters concerning the State.

Through the critical Year of Grace, 1916, when the future of the world's civilisation was trembling in the balance, the Allies lived utterly unsuspicious of this astounding state of affairs. Downing Street and the Quai d'Orsay were in ignorance of the deeply-laid plot of the Emperor William to crush and destroy that splendid piece of patriotic machinery, "the Russian steam-roller." We in England were frantically making munitions for Russia, and lending her the sinews of war, merely regarding the erotic monk as a society tea-drinking buffoon such as one meets in every capital.

The truth has, however, been revealed by the amazing results of diligent inquiries made by that patriotic little band of Russians who united at the end of 1916 to rid the Empire of its most dangerous enemy, and have placed their secret reports in my hands. The Emperor, though exceedingly rancorous, and though in appearance a quiet, inoffensive little man, was yet capable of the utmost cruelty and hardness. He has been responsible for some terrible miscarriages of justice. His callousness is well-known. After the catastrophe of Khodinska, which cost the lives of nearly two thousand of his subjects, he danced the whole night at a ball given by the French Ambassador, while on reading the telegram which told him of the disaster of Tsushima, which cost Russia her whole fleet and the loss of so many precious lives, he made no remark, but continued his game of tennis in the park of Tsarskoe-Selo.

Those of his personal entourage wondered. They asked themselves whether it was stoicism, indifference, or a strength of mind abnormal. It was neither. Throughout the whole career of Nicholas II his only thought had been to flee from danger, and to leave to others the task of pulling the chestnuts from the fire.

Rasputin and his shrewd and clever fellow-traitors knew all this, and were acting upon the Emperor's weaknesses, more especially upon His Majesty's belief in spiritualism and his fear to thwart the imperious declarations of his German-born wife. Alexandra Feodorovna, the complex neurotic woman who had begun her career as Empress by determining to exclude from Court all ladies with blemished reputations, and all those black sheep who creep by back-stair influence into every Court of Europe, had now under Rasputin's influence welcomed any of the monk's lady friends, however tarnished their reputations.

There can be no doubt that the Empress's nerves were not in a sound condition. True, she was in constant communication with Germany, and her actions showed her readiness to betray Russia into the hands of her own people. This fact the world ought to take into consideration. The Empress is the most interesting character-study in the world to-day. We can have no sympathy with those who are traitors, yet it has been clearly proved that the horrors of the Revolution had left a deep impression on her mind. She had no fatalism in her character, and she lived in daily dread of seeing her children and husband murdered. She had no courage. Her highly-strung nature took more seriously to the soothing effect of the evil monk Rasputin's teaching than would the mind of a woman of normal calibre; hence, while "Nikki" her husband believed implicitly in "dear Gregory's" advice, she also believed him to be the heaven-sent deliverer of Russia, to wrest it from disaster, and to give to the poor little Tsarevitch good health as Heir to the Romanoff dynasty.

Those latter days of 1916 were truly strenuous ones in the Imperial household. On December 8th the Emperor had left for Moscow, and to him the Tsaritza telegraphed in their private code, as follows:

Tsarskoe-Selo, December 8th, 11:30 A.M.
"Gregory says that Zakomelsky is proposing a resolution denouncing him at the Council of the Empire to-morrow. At all costs this must be prevented. Boris and Fredericks agree. You must stop it.

Alec

To this there was sent a reply, the copy being on record:

Moscow, December 8th, 10 P.M.
"Quite agree with undesirability of allowing Z. to criticise, but cannot see how I can prevent it, unless by arrest. I am communicating with a certain quarter. Shall return to-morrow.

Nikki

Apparently the Emperor, whatever steps he took, was unable to secure the arrest of the Leader of the Centre, for on the following day, at the meeting of the Council, the resolution was moved by the Baron Meller Zakomelsky, who recognised M. Trepoff's honest and sincere desire to combat the so-called "dark forces," but warned the Prime Minister that the method chosen by him was wrong. The only effective weapon, he said, was light, and the Duma and the Council called on the Government to join them in revealing and denouncing the notorious sinister influence. The whole of Russia awaited the eradication of the plague which was corroding the State organism.

This resolution apparently stirred into action the forces gradually arising to combat the camarilla, for on December 13th, Baroness Mesentzoff, wife of Baron Paul Mesentzoff, chamberlain and councillor of State, and a fair-haired "sister-disciple" of Rasputin's, sent him a letter of warning which is in existence, and of which I here give an English translation.

It was handed to him late at night at his home in the Gorokhovaya. Seated with him in that little sanctum into which his neophytes were admitted by his discreet body-servant, and drinking heavily as usual, were Sturmer, the ex-Premier, and a man named Kartchevsky, a renegade, who was actually at that moment secretary to General von Beseler, the German Governor-General of Warsaw.

The letter read as follows:

Holy Father,

I have been with Anna (Madame Vyrubova) and Olga (the Tsar's daughter) an hour ago. I have told them to warn Her Majesty the Empress of a desperate plot against you. Do beware, I pray you, of Youssoupoff, and of the Grand Duke Dmitri. There is a conspiracy to kill you!

"Your pretended friend Pourichkevitch dined with me to-night, and he, too, intends that you shall be removed. We all pray that no harm shall befall you. But I send this at once in warning. I shall be at the seance tomorrow, when I hope to have an opportunity of speaking with you alone. A young friend of mine, Nadjezda Boldyieff, daughter of the General at Kiev, is anxious to enter our circle. So I shall bring her with me. But do, I beg of you, heed this warning, and avoid all contact with the persons herein named.

Your sister,
Feo

The monk, who was in his cups, as he usually was after midnight—according to his servant's statement—handed the letter to Sturmer with an inane laugh. And stroking his beard, said with his extraordinary egotism:

"Enemies! Why do these silly impetuous women warn me? I am careful enough to look after myself. I rule Russia—at the orders of the Emperor William! The Tsar is only Tsar in name. The Emperor is myself, Gregory the monk!"

"But Pourichkevitch is dangerous," declared the traitorous ex-Prime Minister. "He is the fiercest member of the Extreme Right, and our friend Protopopoff has lately received many reports concerning him through the Secret Police."

"If so, then why is he not imprisoned?" asked Rasputin. "Protopopoff is far too hesitating. A few compromising documents introduced into his house, a police search, an arrest, a word to the Emperor—and he would have an uncomfortable little room beneath the lake in the Fortress of Schusselburg. No, our friend Protopopoff is far too weak. He dallies too much for the public favour. What is it worth? Personally, I prefer their hatred."

"And yet you are the great healer—the idol of the working-class, just as Gapon was long ago!" laughed the ex-Premier.

"Yes, I am their Grichka," laughed Rasputin in his drunken humour. "It is true, my dear Boris. There is but one Tsar, and it is myself—eh?" And he chuckled as he drained his glass of champagne, and laughed at the warning sent him by the woman who had sat at his knee and who had given over her whole private fortune to him, just as a dozen other society women in Petrograd had done. If his "sister-disciples" failed him in funds, then he simply held their letters and blackmailed them till he drove them to desperation, and in six known cases to suicide. The fears of the Empress Alexandra Feodorovna for the safety of her pet monk in whom she believed so devoutly, seem to have been aroused by the warning given by the Baroness Mesentzoff, for next day there came to him an urgent telegram from Gatchina, where the Tsaritza had gone on a visit to the Dowager Empress. It read:

"You are in grave danger. Mother Superior Paula, of the
Novo-Devitsky Nunnery, has disclosed something to me.
Come to Tsarskoe-Selo at once. Nikki is eager to consult you.

A.

The monk was quick to realise by this telegram his true position in the Imperial household. Only a few weeks before Anna Vyrubova, the high-priestess of his disgraceful cult, had warned him of his waning influence. But he had not cared one jot, because, in his safe, he had stowed hundreds of letters and telegrams from society women compromising themselves. By the sale of these he could obtain sufficient money to establish a fortune for the rest of his life.

Here, however, a new phase had arisen.

He was in active communication with Germany, he had already wrecked Russia's splendid offensive, and was gradually bringing the Empire into bad odour with neutrals. For this he had, in secret, received the heartfelt thanks of his Imperial paymaster the Kaiser. German money was flowing to him from all quarters, and German agents were swarming in Petrograd, as well as across the Russian front. Brusiloff was doing his best, but having gauged the position, had realised that it was becoming hopeless. German influence was eating the heart out of Russia as a canker-worm—and that canker-worm was Gregory Rasputin himself.

In consequence of the telegram from the Empress, followed by a letter sent by Imperial messenger by the Grand Duchess Olga, the monk hastened to the Palace and had a long interview with Her Majesty.

He left with Anna Vyrubova soon after noon in one of the Imperial cars which were always at his disposal, in consequence of the seance arranged at his house in Petrograd, and more especially because the Baroness Mesentzoff had sent him a photograph of Nadjezda Boldyieff, who was anxious to join the "disciples."

Notwithstanding the critical situation, the seance was held, and the handsome Nadjezda was admitted to the "sisterhood."

Truly those were critical days in Russia. The rascal had been warned, but did not heed. The Allies, fighting for the just cause, were in ignorance of the fierce resentment now aroused in the hearts of the Russian people by the denunciation in the Duma by those who were bold enough to speak their minds and defy the camarilla. The news allowed out of Russia during the last month of the year was most meagre. Protopopoff, the Kaiser's silk-hatted creature, controlled it, and only allowed intelligence of the most optimistic character to filter through to us. Hence while the British, American, and French Press were publishing wholly fictitious accounts of Russia's gains, the "miracle-worker" was daily driving the Imperial House of Romanoff towards the abyss of oblivion.

XII

The True Story of Rasputin's End

E vents were now proceeding apace.

The Grand Duke Nicholas Michailovitch had dared to seek audience of the Tsar, at which he had handed him a memorandum of protest. In this letter, which is still upon record, the Grand Duke wrote:

> "Where is the root of the evil? Let me explain it in a few words.
>
> "So long as your manner of choosing Ministers was known to narrow circles, things could muddle along, but when it became a matter of public knowledge and all classes in Russia talked about it, it was senseless to attempt to continue to govern Russia in this fashion. Often did you tell me that you could put faith in no one, and that you were being deceived.
>
> "If this is so, then it applies particularly to your wife, who loves you and yet led you into error, being surrounded by evil-minded intimates. You believe in Alexandra Feodorovna. This is natural. But the words she utters are the product of skilful machinations, not of truth. If you are powerless to liberate her from these influences, then at all events be on your guard against constant and systematic influence of intriguers who are using your wife as their instrument. . . If you could remove the persistent interference of dark forces in all matters, the regeneration of Russia would instantly be advanced, and you would regain the confidence of the enormous majority of your subjects, which you have forfeited."

This was pretty outspoken. But further, during the course of the conversation, the Grand Duke spoke of Protopopoff and asked Nicholas II whether he was aware that this politician had been palmed off on him by the agency of Rasputin, whom Protopopoff had first met at the home of the charlatan Badmayeff, the man who secretly practised so-called "Thibetan" medicine and who supplied the "Saint" with his drugs.

The Emperor smiled and declared that he was already acquainted with the facts.

The Emperor took the memorandum to the Empress and read it aloud to her. When he came to the passage dealing with the evil influences surrounding her, she flew into a rage, seized the document, and tore it up in the Tsar's face!

Meanwhile the camarilla were still plotting further the downfall of Russia, and endeavouring to implicate Sturmer's successor.

Suddenly, on December 26th, the greatest consternation was caused both in society circles in Petrograd and at the Palace of Tsarskoe-Selo, owing to rumours that Rasputin was missing.

He had been absent from the capital on many occasions, travelling upon his supposed pilgrimages, but there was persistent gossip on the Nevski that something had happened.

After the *debacle* three telegrams in English were found in the Department of Posts and Telegraphs. They had been sent by the Empress from Tsarskoe-Selo to the Emperor, and read as follows:

Tsarskoe-Selo, December 26th
"I am worried by the awful rumours. No details. Remember what I wrote to you.

Alec

Four days later Her Majesty telegraphed again to the Tsar:

Tsarskoe-Selo, December 30th, 4:37 P.M.
"Can you send Voyeipoff to me at once? I want his help and advice. We still hope for the best. Dmitri and Felix are implicated.

Alec

Six hours later she again telegraphed frantically:

Tsarskoe-Selo, December 30th, 10:24 P.M.
"Nothing discovered yet. Felix stopped on his way to Crimea. How I wish you were here.

Alec

And again at midnight she sent two further telegrams. The first read:

Tsarskoe-Selo, December 30th, 11:47 P.M.
"Father (Rasputin) is no more. Punish the enemies of Russia
and of our House. Come back at once. I can bear it no longer.

Alec

The second was addressed:

To Father Makarius, Verkhotursky Monastery, Perm
December 30th, midnight
"Great misfortune. Something happened to Father (Rasputin).
Pray for him and for us. Those responsible will be punished.
Come at once to us.

Alexandra

For days the sensational affair was hushed-up from the public
by order of the Tsar, and with the connivance of Protopopoff. Many
fictitious accounts have appeared in the Press regarding the final hours
of the amazing rascal who, as tool of the Emperor William, brought to
an end the Imperial House of Romanoff.

I am here enabled, however, to explain the truth from an authentic
source, namely, from the statement of a lady—a Russian nursing-
sister—who was an eye-witness and who is in London at the moment
when I write. The lady in question is well known in London, and I have
begged her to allow me to disclose her name, but for certain reasons she
has held me to my promise of secrecy. There are, one must remember,
still influential friends of Rasputin in Russia, and as she is returning
there, her objection is obvious.

It seems that on December 15th (Russian style) the "Saint" had
been invited to the elegant house of Prince Youssoupoff to a merry
supper. The *penchant* of the monk for a pretty face and a mysterious
adventure being well-known, it had been hinted to him that a certain
lady who desired to remain incognito, wished to meet him.

Now the house of Prince Youssoupoff in Petrograd—who, by the
way, had a house in London before the war and was well-known in
Mayfair—runs from the Moskaya to the Offitzerskaya, where at a back
entrance, the wine from the famous estate in the Crimea is sold, just as
wine is sold at the mediaeval palaces of Florence.

The Prince was supposed to be alone to meet his guest and this
mysterious young and pretty lady who desired to enter the cult of the

"Sister-Disciples." As a matter of fact, however, there were assembled in a room on the first floor several persons determined to rid Russia of this erotic traitor who was daily betraying her into the hands of the Huns.

They were the Prince Youssoupoff, the Grand Duke Dmitri (who was suspected by the Empress), the Deputy of the Extreme Right, Pourichkevitch, a man named Stepanoff, a well-known *danseuse* (the mysterious lady who acted as decoy, named Mademoiselle C—), and the lady who has described the scene to me.

Eleven o'clock struck. It was a dramatic scene. All were anxious for Rasputin's arrival, but he did not come.

The Prince went to the telephone and asked for the monk at his house.

The reply was that the Father had gone out to dine somewhere early in the evening.

Would he come? Would he walk into the trap so cunningly baited for him?

The moments seemed hours as the little assembly sat waiting and discussing whether any one could have given him warning, for it was known that the "miracle-worker" had, through his catspaw Protopopoff, spies set everywhere.

At twenty minutes past eleven a car was heard at the back-door in the Offitzerskaya, and his host, rushing down, admitted him mysteriously. The monk removed his big sable-lined coat, disclosing his black clerical garb and big bejewelled cross suspended around his neck. Then he removed his galoshes, for it was snowing hard outside.

"You need not be afraid, Father," said his host. "We are alone, except for my friend Stepanoff. He is one of us," he laughed merrily.

Then he conducted the "Saint" into the large handsome dining-room, where a tall, fair-bearded man, Paul Stepanoff, came forward to meet him.

Upon the table were two bottles of wine. Into one cyanide of potassium had been introduced, and its potency had an hour before been tried upon a dog, which at the moment was lying dead in the yard outside.

After Stepanoff had been introduced, the Prince said in a confidential tone:

"The lady I mentioned has not yet arrived. I shall go to the door to await her so that the servants are not disturbed."

Thus the Father was left with his merry, easy-going fellow-guest, who at a glance he saw was a *bon viveur* like himself.

The two men began to talk of spiritualism, in which Stepanoff declared himself to be much interested, and a few minutes later he poured out some wine, filling the Father's glass from the poisoned bottle while he attracted his attention to a picture at the end of the room.

They raised their glasses, and drank. Some dry biscuits were in a silver box, and after Rasputin had drained his glass, he took a biscuit and munched it.

But to Stepanoff's amazement the poison took no effect! Was the monk after all under some divine or mysterious protection? Stepanoff was expecting him to be seized by paroxysms of agony every moment.

On the contrary, he was still calm and expectant regarding the mysterious lady whom he was to meet.

Suddenly, however, Rasputin, slightly paler than usual, exclaimed: "Curious! I do not feel very well!"

And he crossed the room to examine an ancient crucifix, beautifully jewelled, which was standing upon a side table.

Stepanoff rose and followed him, remarking on the beauty of the sacred emblem, yet aghast that the "Saint" could take such a dose of poison and yet remain unharmed.

Prince Youssoupoff with the others, was standing silent in the upstairs room eagerly awaiting Stepanoff's announcement that the traitor was no more. Those moments were breathless ones. What, they wondered, was happening below! They listened, and could hear the voices of the pair below still in conversation.

"Ah! That spasm has passed!" Rasputin was heard to declare.

Passed! Was he immune from the effects of that most deadly poison? They looked at each other astounded. The fact was that he had only sipped the wine, and having had sufficient already to drink he had contrived to empty his glass into a dark porcelain flower-bowl.

The monk had taken the big crucifix in his hand to examine it the more closely, when Stepanoff, seeing that Rasputin was still unharmed suddenly drew a big Browning pistol, and, placing it under the monk's arm and against his breast, fired.

The others above, hearing the shot, rushed out upon the wide balcony, while Stepanoff dashed up the stairs to meet them, crying:

"The Saint is dead at last! Russia is freed of the scoundrel!"

The others shouted joy, and re-entering the room, toasted the liberation and regeneration of Russia. Suddenly, they heard a noise and went out upon the balcony again, when, to their horror, they saw the door of the dining-room opened, and Rasputin, haggard and blood-stained, staggering forth, with an imprecation upon his lips, to the door opening to the street, in an effort to escape!

The attempt at poisoning him had failed, and he had only been wounded.

The tension was breathless. Was he after all endowed with some supernatural power?

"You have tried to kill me!" shrieked the monk, his hands stained with blood. "But I still live—I live!—and God will give me my revenge!" With his hands clasped over the spot where he had been wounded, he gave vent to a peal of demoniacal laughter, which held the little knot of witnesses on the balcony utterly dumbfounded and appalled.

Only one man seemed to have courage to stir.

According to the lady who was present and who gives me the description which I here reproduce—the only true and authentic account of the affair—Stepanoff, his revolver still in his hand, again dashed down the stairs, and preventing the monk from opening the outer door, sprang upon him and emptied the contents of his weapon, barrel after barrel, into the monk's head.

At last the spy and traitor was dead!

Ten minutes later a closed car arrived containing Doctor Stanislas L—, and driven by a soldier in uniform named Ivan F—. In the car the body of the monk was placed by the doctor, the soldier, and the patriotic executioner Stepanoff.

Leaving the Prince and those who had assembled to witness the death of the hated agent of the Kaiser who had so misled the Russian Imperial family and the Russian people, and who had been directly and indirectly responsible for the death of thousands of brave men, British and French, on the various battle-fronts, the men drove with the fellow's body, the great golden cross still dangling around its neck, to the Petrovsky Bridge.

It was very dark and snowy. Nobody was about, therefore the doctor, the soldier, and the man who had that night lopped off the tentacle of the German octopus in Russia, carried the body to a point between the second and third arches of the bridge. Here it had been ascertained earlier in the night that the ice was broken, and a large hole existed.

They raised the body to cast it over when, horror! The dead hand caught in the soldier's shoulder-strap!

"Is this a curse upon me?" gasped Ivan.

"Curse or not, he goes!" cried Stepanoff, and all three hurled him over the parapet.

There was a loud splash. Then all was silent again, and the trio, re-entering the car, drove hurriedly away.

For six days there were rumours everywhere in Petrograd that "something" had happened. Fredericks, Sturmer, and Protopopoff were frantic. The Secret Police, at orders of the Emperor, were making every inquiry, for the Holy Father was missing!

On December 31st, at 3 P.M., the Tsaritza despatched the following telegram to Nicholas II.

"Order Maksimovitch arrest Dmitri (the Grand Duke) in your name. Dmitri waited to see me to-day. I refused. The body has not yet been found.—Alec."

To this His Majesty replied that he was taking every measure, and that he had ordered the Grand Duke Nicholas into exile to his estates.

Then, on the following day, the distracted Empress, who was grief-stricken and inconsolable at the tragedy, telegraphed "Thanks for your wire. Body found in the river."

An abandoned motor-car soaked in blood had been found miles out of the city. It was believed to belong to a Grand Duke. The entire police and detective force of the capital had in the meantime been afoot, and raked through all the houses of ill-fame, gipsy singers' haunts, and in fact every conceivable place, until the finding of a blood-stained galosh, proved to have belonged to Rasputin, gave evidence of a tragedy.

The ice on the river and canals was, of course, several feet thick, but it is the custom in Russia to cut openings where water is obtained and linen is rinsed by laundresses. Divers went down, but discovered nothing; eventually, however, the body was picked up near the bank, not far from where it had been thrown in.

When it was discovered the Empress saw it in secret and knelt before it, crying hysterically for half-an-hour. Anna Vyrubova standing in silence at her side.

Then, at the Empress's orders, it was buried privately and at night at Tsarskoe-Selo.

In the meantime the Emperor had arrived post-haste from the front, and for three days extremely guarded references to an "interesting murder" appeared in the Petrograd and foreign Press. Alongside were printed some biographical notes regarding the chief actors in the tragedy. No mention, however, was allowed to be made of Rasputin.

Suddenly, however, the public were told that the notorious monk had "ended his life." But nothing was said as to when or by what means.

Thus closed the infamous career of the dark force in Russia, and by the tragedy the whole amazing truth which I have here disclosed became revealed. The secret plotting of Germany, and the using of the mock-monk to sap the power of Russia's offensive, will live ever in history, and will, no doubt, be the theme of many future historians. But all will agree that the words of the weak, neurotic Empress, when she was told by Anna Vyrubova of Rasputin's death, were prophetic.

"Dead!" she gasped, her face blanched to the lips. "If the Holy Father is dead, then, alas! the Dynasty of the Romanoffs is dead also!"

Those words of hers were true indeed, for within three months the Tsar had signed his abdication, and the Imperial pair, together with the camarilla of traitors, were prisoners in the hands of those who intended that Russia should yet be re-born and freed of its Teuton taint, and of the disgraceful cult of that blasphemous and scheming rascal Rasputin.

The End

A Note About the Author

William Le Queux (1864–1927) was an Anglo-French journalist, novelist, and radio broadcaster. Born in London to a French father and English mother, Le Queux studied art in Paris and embarked on a walking tour of Europe before finding work as a reporter for various French newspapers. Towards the end of the 1880s, he returned to London where he edited *Gossip* and *Piccadilly* before being hired as a reporter for *The Globe* in 1891. After several unhappy years, he left journalism to pursue his creative interests. Le Queux made a name for himself as a leading writer of popular fiction with such espionage thrillers as *The Great War in England in 1897* (1894) and *The Invasion of 1910* (1906). In addition to his writing, Le Queux was a notable pioneer of early aviation and radio communication, interests he maintained while publishing around 150 novels over his decades long career.

A Note from the Publisher

Spanning many genres, from non-fiction essays to literature classics to children's books and lyric poetry, Mint Edition books showcase the master works of our time in a modern new package. The text is freshly typeset, is clean and easy to read, and features a new note about the author in each volume. Many books also include exclusive new introductory material. Every book boasts a striking new cover, which makes it as appropriate for collecting as it is for gift giving. Mint Edition books are only printed when a reader orders them, so natural resources are not wasted. We're proud that our books are never manufactured in excess and exist only in the exact quantity they need to be read and enjoyed. To learn more and view our library, go to minteditionbooks.com

bookfinity & MINT EDITIONS

Enjoy more of your favorite classics with Bookfinity,
a new search and discovery experience for readers.
With Bookfinity, you can discover more vintage
literature for your collection, find your Reader Type,
track books you've read or want to read,
and add reviews to your favorite books.
Visit www.bookfinity.com, and click on
Take the Quiz to get started.

Don't forget to follow us
@bookfinityofficial and @mint_editions

CPSIA information can be obtained
at www.ICGtesting.com
Printed in the USA
BVHW092244110621
609354BV00006B/1727

9 781513 277806